GO, GO, GO,
SAID THE BIRD

GO, GO, GO, SAID
THE BIRD

HUMAN KIND'S UNBEARABLE
REALITIES – AND WHAT MIGHT BE
GAINED BY ACCEPTING THEM

RICHARD OERTON

2024 ?

Troubador Publishing Ltd
Unit E2 Airfield Business Park
Harrison Road, Market Harborough
Leicestershire LE16 7UL
Tel: 0116 279 2299
Email: books@troubador.co.uk
Web: www.troubador.co.uk

ISBN 978-1-83628-101-6

British Library Cataloguing in Publication Data.
A catalogue record for this book is available from the British Library.

Printed and bound by CPI Group (UK) Ltd, Croydon, CR0 4YY
Typeset in 11.5pt Minion Pro by Troubador Publishing Ltd, Leicester, UK

MIX
Paper | Supporting
responsible forestry
FSC® C013604
FSC
www.fsc.org

Go, go, go, said the bird: human kind
Cannot bear very much reality.

T.S. Eliot, *Four Quartets* (Burnt Norton)

Facts do not cease to exist
because they are ignored.

Aldous Huxley, Proper Studies, 1927

I have laboured carefully, not to
mock, lament, or execrate human
actions, but to understand them.

Baruch Spinoza, Political Treatise, 1677

Contents

Preface

On 5 November 2023, *The Observer* newspaper devoted most of its front page to proposals, prepared by officials acting for a cabinet minister, that the definition of extremism should be widened. The new definition would say:

> Extremism is the promotion or advancement of any ideology which aims to overturn or undermine the UK's system of parliamentary democracy, its institutions and values.

I've done a lot of legal drafting in my time and the lawyer in me elbows the rest of me aside in order to point to ambiguities in this definition. Grammatically, it looks as if the institutions and values might be those of the system of parliamentary democracy, rather than those of the UK, but I don't think that interpretation was intended. And then I wonder whether the penultimate word should be "or" instead of "and". Must the ideology aim to do all these three things if it is to be extreme? Does it really escape this label if, for example, it aims to overturn our institutions and values while leaving our parliamentary democracy intact – a scenario worth considering because if our values and institutions really were overturned, there would be no need to undermine democracy as well: the overturning would be reflected automatically in what and who we voted for.

This pedantry aside, however, the thrust of the definition seems fairly clear, and it was widely criticised as an attack on free speech. What strikes me more forcibly, however, is that it is an attack on *change*. There is built into it the assumption that our institutions and values, as they existed in November 2023, cannot be bettered and must always be preserved. Consider what the effect would have been if this definition had existed in earlier times – different times when there were, among our institutions, slavery, bear bating, the burning of witches and heretics and a system of parliamentary democracy that denied the vote to women; and, among our values, the received wisdom that homosexuality was evil, that children might be labelled illegitimate, that public hangings for theft were morally right and that suicides should be buried at a crossroads with stakes through their bodies. I learned only the other day that, among the institutions in fifteenth century Scotland, was the burial while still alive of epileptic women who became pregnant.

On the whole, I have not been fortunate in those who had charge of me at my several schools, but I was fortunate in Mr Pond, who taught me when I was about twelve or thirteen and persuaded the headmaster (in whom I was not at all fortunate) to introduce several alternatives to the playing of games. It may have been he who required my class to learn by heart the passage in Tennyson's *Morte d'Arthur* that begins:

And slowly answered Arthur from the barge:
"The old order changeth, yielding place to new,
And God fulfils Himself in many ways,
Lest one good custom should corrupt the world ..."

I remember rather liking this, although I didn't fully understand it, and at the time I was not bothered by the changing of old orders being attributed to God. Mr Pond himself was fortunate because he fell in love with the school matron, Miss Flood, and they went off to found a better school of their own.

I like to think that, within the spirit if not the letter of the definition, I am myself an extremist. I don't want to overturn or undermine parliamentary democracy (even though it could probably be improved, and it certainly leads too often to government by fools or knaves or people who are just deeply unpleasant), but I do hope for the day when our species faces up to some unbearable realities and, in doing so, sees that many of our present institutions and values really are in need of change. To preserve them intact is for us to condemn ourselves to continuing error and incomprehension, and to a degree of suffering which is unnecessary and unjustifiable.

This book takes its title from a line of T.S. Eliot's *Four Quartets* and I have tried to bring Eliot into it here and there, but in writing about the realities that humankind cannot at present bear I have chosen some of those that weigh on my own mind and are almost certainly not the ones that he himself was thinking of (if indeed he was thinking of any in particular). As it is, the book pays rather more attention to one reality – the non-existence of what we call free will, and the consequences of letting it go – than to others. And here I must offer an apology. I've already produced two short books on this subject and some people have bought them and may actually have read them. If any of this select band should happen to read the present book they would find some of the same things being said. I can only apologise for any irritation this may cause, and for any sense of being short-changed.

M ⚊ F + the local 14
1950

W +

b 1936

CPA at school + H

BF
a ℓ

+ suicide

ONE

Something of myself

I was three years old when the Second World War began, and when I went to West Bank nursery school I was required for the first time to join in prayers. I found that they all ended with "Amen" – pronounced "ah-men" rather than "ay-men". In trying to make sense of this word, I heard it as "our men". Forces fighting for the Allies were often referred to in this way, and I supposed that all prayers ended with this tribute to them.

The war permeated much of what I remember of my childhood. Many of the things we couldn't do were things we might be able to do "after the war". One of these things was to have a holiday far from home. I lived with my parents in north Devon, and the best we could do was to spend a few days at a hotel just down the coast in Bude. I went with my mother (I was an only child), but sometimes my father took a little time off from being a solicitor and joined us. I rather liked Bude because you could hire boats to row on the canal, and I found to my surprise that I was quite good at rowing.

One evening the hotel arranged a special event. A small, elderly and quietly spoken man, who nonetheless seemed confident of his worth, came to perform what he described as "sketches". I remember nothing of these, and I probably failed to understand them, but at one point there was some task to be done – perhaps it had to do with counting – in which he invited all the children present to take part. The other children in the audience jumped up obediently and went to do whatever it was. I stayed in my seat and watched them. Perhaps it had not occurred to me that I was included in this invitation; more likely I knew that I was but was afraid to accept it. The small man said to me accusingly, "Aren't you going to join them?", and so I did, but I was reluctant and took no part in the project.

I mention this incident because of the way it portrays me: as someone different, an outsider, not a joiner, someone detached, unconfident to the point of being fearful, not easy in his skin or easy among others or easy in the world. Throughout my life, I think I have remained that person. Sometimes my confidence has grown, and sometimes I have supposed that I felt like everyone else. Sometimes, too, I have compensated for my feeling of insecurity by being rather arrogant and unkind. But I have always known that this debilitating version of myself waited in the wings and often stepped forward to take part in the action on the stage or to disrupt it. I am not concerned here with how I came to be like this. I mention it only because I think it opened the way for me to think the thoughts that I try to express in this book. My late wife had, as her criterion for right behaviour, the idea of what "most people do" – a criterion shared, by definition, with most people – and it was sad for us both that I never shared it with her. Conformity for its own sake has not appealed to me, and received wisdom has never seemed worthy of receipt without being questioned. For this I claim no credit and accept no discredit.

Barbara Wootton, who became, as one of the first life peeresses, Baroness Wootton of Abinger, was something of a polymath: a sociologist, a socialist, an economist, a criminologist, a magistrate, a penal reformer ... and in the latter guise she appears in my penultimate chapter. Among the many books she wrote – and she wrote beautifully – was an autobiographical one called *In a World I Never Made.* Its title is a line from A.E. Houseman's poem, *The laws of God, the laws of man,* and when you add the previous line it reads:

> I, a stranger and afraid
> In a world I never made.

I myself identify rather strongly with this poem, but I am a little surprised that she did. Once long ago she invited me to visit her in the House of Lords. Although nervous because I felt hugely honoured, I thought we got on fairly well, and she suggested that after lunch I might like to watch proceedings in the Chamber. I agreed enthusiastically. Then two things happened. To end our lunch we had strawberries, and to make conversation I said that my wife happened to be suffering from a complete loss of taste, brought about by some infection, and that this made me feel a little guilty for enjoying them so much. She found this throwaway remark completely baffling: she could not understand why I should have made it, and it seemed to disturb her. She was still more disturbed when I expressed an interest in psychoanalysis. This put the tin lid on it. She cancelled her invitation to show me the Chamber – "some other time", she said – and soon after that we parted company. Perhaps she was upset because she took both my remarks as evidence of irrationality on my part (or at least, in the case of psychoanalysis, of an interest in the irrational) and irrationality was anathema to her. And it's true, I suppose, that her whole career was a demonstration of rationality, but surely it must have taken its inspiration from something quite different: from a wholly emotional urge, as a reformer, to remake the world that she had never made, remoulding it nearer to the heart's desire.

I regretted the outcome of our meeting very much, and our relationship soon deteriorated still further. I was at the time the book review editor of the *Howard Journal* – the journal of the Howard League for Penal Reform – and she had kindly agreed to review a book. The then Secretary of the Howard League, Hugh Klare, was keen to build up a library and to that end he asked book reviewers to return the books after reviewing them. He went so far as to write "Howard League Library" on the flyleaves. Barbara Wootton was very angry on seeing this: "I've got a bone to pick with you", she said, and added that she had agreed to review the book only because she wanted to keep it. I tried to explain that none of this was of my doing, but she was fed up with me by then.

I put a lot of work into obtaining and editing the book reviews in the *Howard Journal*, writing some myself, and I suppose I learned a certain amount about crime in the process, but I was never very good at it. I was given a list of potential reviewers, and I started badly by asking one of them to review a book of which he was himself an editor. Some reviewers had to be chased mercilessly to send the reviews which they had agreed to write. Into this category fell a senior Home Office official whose reviews were very valuable but harder than teeth to extract from her. Into a very different category fell the Reverend W.J. Bolt. He was a joy. He would review almost anything, and his reviews were always thoughtful, well-judged, and – above all – on time. I didn't get on well with Hugh Klare's right-hand woman, who was in charge of the League's administrative work. I regret this now because I think my defensive arrogance came into play and I didn't behave well. I had a bad stammer, which has stayed with me throughout my life until it has eased off in old age, and she said she found this hard to cope with, as indeed did I. She once had me described, on the cover of an issue of the Journal, as the Revue Editor, but I think it would be wrong to see this as an act of revenge on her part.

At this time I had been qualified for some years as a solicitor, and these experiences must seem out of key with that state. The truth is that, in one respect at least, I rather resembled Reginald Hine, who described his own work as a solicitor as "doing my duty in a state of life into which it had *not* pleased God to call me". Born in 1883, Hine practised as a solicitor in Hitchin, Hertfordshire – but very reluctantly because he really wanted to be a full-time man of letters, an antiquarian and a historian. He wrote several books on the history of Hitchin, met many writers, and was justly famous in his time for his book, *Confessions of an Un-Common Attorney*. In 1949, after a spat with his fellow solicitors had been taken up for adjudication by the Law Society, he broke off a conversation with someone on a railway station seat, got up abruptly and threw himself in front of an oncoming train. As a young man he worked as a newspaper reporter, and he records a visit to a house in the slums of Hitchin to report on the death of a soldier in the First World War:

> There were three generations in this house, in two rooms. The telegram that morning brought news of the death of the father of six or so children who were there. They were the third generation and were seated on broken boxes and chairs round a bed on which newspapers were spread. They were having their tea. There was no table – the bed had to do for that. I got my facts and the inevitable photograph from the fly-blown frame and was given every help by the widow, but it was an experience I have never forgotten. The bed that served as a tea-table was occupied by the father of

the soldier who had been killed. He, too, was dead, but there seemed nowhere else to put the body so it was left in the bed and the tea was served around it.

These children would have been only middle-aged when I was born.

Dejectedly, I was a boarder at a mildly-upper-range public school. Beating was a regular feature, done by prefects who ran very nearly the length of the cloisters to add impetus to their blows, the resulting bruises going deep and taking weeks to fade. (It's interesting to reflect that if this damage were done to a child today, and done by a parent, the child would probably be taken into care.) My father died when I was fourteen, my scholastic record was not outstanding, my sporting record was outstandingly bad, and I was eased out of school at the age of sixteen by my housemaster, a scholar of Greek and a bachelor who should never have been allowed within sight of growing boys, some of whom might be in need of help and encouragement. I left with mixed feelings, sad to be thought unworthy of further education and with a lasting feeling of disqualification, but very glad to be rid of the place, and (whether for this or other reasons) with a certain lasting sympathy for people whom luck has not favoured.

I came from a family of solicitors – dead and alive, there are seven of us now – and for want of any other calling I joined a family firm as an articled clerk and found that I was much better at learning the law than I had been at learning school subjects. A university degree was unnecessary in those days and I went on to qualify, but my legal career has been atypical, largely because of my stammer and its implications. And although it has been quite absorbing at times (I spent thirteen years at the Law Commission) I have always felt, as Hine did, albeit for different reasons, that it wasn't really for me.

6

I have always supposed that to be a writer – a real writer – must be to lead a life of fabulous adventure, not in the world but in the mind, and that the next best thing was to make an adventure out of reading. So I read quite a lot, perhaps trying unconsciously to reduce the feeling of disqualification with which my early ejection from school had left me. This may account for my involvement with the Howard League – and for much else, including my rebellion against some of the assumptions that characterised my profession. My early interest in psychoanalysis, both in theory and in practice, led me at one stage to become briefly acquainted with Edward Glover, both a psychiatrist and one of the early British analysts. (He was a classical Freudian who had no truck at all with the work of Melanie Klein, which had caused a split within the British Psychoanalytical Society.) I had read a couple of his books and when I wrote to him he replied with extraordinary kindness and almost at once diagnosed my problem by asking, "Why did you become a solicitor?" I can't remember how I replied. Had I been honest, I should have had to admit that cowardice was a part of the answer. He also said, "The time will come when you will enter into your kingdom", a forecast that cheered me up at the time, but one that was less perceptive and has not been validated by events.

I've mentioned having sympathy – empathy might be a better word – with those whom Donald Trump would describe as losers. My son, who was a forensic clinical psychologist, said he felt as though he had one skin fewer than other people and was less able to shrug off the world's pain as others did. I suppose I have felt rather the same. When I lived in Belsize Park, close to the Hampstead Heath I loved, something happened that haunted me. A young boy, exploring as boys do, tried to climb into a deserted building from its roof by sliding down some sort of ventilation shaft. It was a dead end. He couldn't get into the building and he couldn't get out again. No one knew where he was. His body was found by chance years later. If I'd had the right number of skins, perhaps I should have dismissed this from my mind as just another tragedy, and then perhaps I should not have had to imagine his feelings during the days that it took him to die. "Pity is cruel. Pity destroys", Graham Greene said.

My son died, too. Ostensibly it was a long and deep clinical depression that made him kill himself, but he might have survived if he had had the right number of skins. Although he died one morning on the stairs in his house, with a belt around his neck, he had put on his overcoat as if he were going on a journey. Nowadays I try to avoid reading about new and improved treatments for depression, because they show that he might have been saved.

My son's best friend – "like a brother to me", my son said – was a young psychiatrist who asked to give an address at his funeral. We did not discuss what he would say, and when the time came he read out Rudyard Kipling's poem, *If.* Perhaps I should have cringed less than I did, because there's a lot to be said for the poem, but at the time it seemed hackneyed and inappropriate. And I had another reason for disliking it because I was once told by my father to learn it by heart. I was far too young to do so, I didn't know how to start, and I was genuinely worried about the likely consequences of my failure. In the event, I think the whole thing was quietly forgotten. But my father was a huge enthusiast for Kipling, attending dinners in his honour, and I'm afraid I disliked the poem on that score too. And yet … very astute and literary readers may have noticed that the heading of this chapter is stolen from Kipling, whose unfinished autobiography, *Something of Myself*, was published in 1937.

This chapter is something of an apologia for the rest of the book, but that's quite enough about me: more than enough, you may say. Now let's look at some realities about human beings in general – realities which, at this stage or our evolution, we can't bear to face but which, at some later stage, we just might manage to accept. To do so would enhance our dignity, our understanding, our kindness and perhaps even our happiness. There's no objective criterion according to which I can show that this would be a good thing to happen. But I don't doubt that it would.

TWO

Rationality

Humankind lays claim to rationality. A reality that we find it hard to bear is that this claim is exaggerated almost to the point of falsity. Bertrand Russell said:

> Man is a rational animal. So at least we have been told. Throughout a long life I have searched diligently for evidence in favour of this statement, but so far I have not had the good fortune to come across it.

The purpose of this chapter is respectfully to endorse and enlarge upon this verdict and to set the scene for some chapters still to come. I owe to T.S. Eliot the title of this book, so let me quote from his poem, *Mr. Apollinax*, about Bertrand Russell lecturing in America:

> I heard the beat of the centaur's hoofs over the hard turf
> As his dry and passionate talk devoured the afternoon.
> "He is a charming man" – "But after all what did he mean?"

In this case what Russell must have meant was not that human beings possess no rationality at all – he would have claimed some for himself and, in writing this book, I suppose I'm claiming a little for myself, too – but rather that they seldom order their lives by means of such rationality as they have.

Among the many important truths about rationality –

reason, rational thought – the most important may be the fact that it is not itself a motive force within the personality. No one has ever been *motivated* by rationality itself to do or to refrain from doing anything. What motivates us is, for want of a better word, emotion – the desires, drives, feelings, needs, ambitions, inhibitions, likes and dislikes which well up within us and upon which we act. Rationality is a tool, something that we use when we want to use it and leave in the toolbox when we don't. It is always, but always and only, employed when we have an emotional wish to employ it – when we need to employ it for an emotionally-motivated purpose.

Perhaps you have an immediate wish to challenge this assertion. Surely, you may say, there are many situations in which rationality prompts us to act. If we are about to rob a bank and we receive a tip-off that the police are inside waiting for us, it is rationality that makes us refrain and drive away quickly. But no: what motivates us to drive away is the emotional desire to avoid being caught and punished. Driving away is the rational means of fulfilling that desire. And this is perhaps the place to make the obvious point that rationality may be employed for bad purposes as well as for good: a lot of rationality must have gone into the planning of the Holocaust.

Is it rational to want to stay alive? No. To preserve the human race, to have children, to love and be loved, to live happily and hopefully, to do good things or to do bad things? No, of course not. There is nothing rational about any of these basic desires. Rationality may help us to fulfil them, but rationality does not dictate them. David Hume, in his *Treatise on Human Nature*, put it like this:

> Reason is, and ought to be, the slave of the passions, and can never pretend to any other office than to serve and obey them.

Not only does our capacity for rational thought lie dormant unless and until we wish to make use of it but, even when we do, it forces nothing upon us. We may still ignore or falsify the conclusions to which it leads and, if we are using it not to reach a quick one-off conclusion but rather to forge a chain of reasoning, each link in the chain requires a continuing emotional commitment. If (to strain the metaphor) we don't like the way it is developing, or the conclusions to which it seems to be leading, we may stop or divert it. And we may do all these things without any conscious awareness of doing them. If you make a statement which is prefaced (expressly or implicitly) by the words, "I think ...", the chances are that it would be prefaced more accurately by, "I feel ...".

Using a very simple and elementary rationality to reach what I have called quick one-off conclusions is something that nearly all of us do nearly all the time, probably without noticing. Suppose that I have moved to a new town and I want to go out for a meal – either Indian or Chinese, I don't mind very much, but I do rather prefer Chinese. Wanting the meal is purely emotional: there is no rationality involved so far. But I do some research and find that there are restaurants of both varieties about the same distance from my home. That's a bit of rationality. At this point I'm likely, in the light of my emotional preference, to opt for the Chinese. But I conceive an emotional desire to pursue my rational researches and I discover other facts: perhaps car parking (if I go by car) is much easier at the Indian restaurant; but perhaps the owner of that restaurant is a local councillor of a political persuasion that I dislike; but perhaps the menu (when I see it online) is very good at the Indian and not so good at the Chinese; but perhaps the online reviews of the Chinese are nonetheless better than those of the Indian; but perhaps the proprietor of the Chinese has been accused (although perhaps subsequently acquitted) of serving cat instead of chicken; but perhaps the prices at the Indian seem (when I look more closely at the menu) to be extortionate; and so on. Any or all of these bits of factual knowledge, revealed through rational investigation, may evoke in me emotional reactions which push me in one direction or the other. Or I may find it all so confusing that I decide to get some fish and chips instead.

This brief scenario is meant to illustrate the way in which we run our everyday lives. The rationality we employ is simple and undemanding and we certainly don't notice, as we go along, that we are dipping and diving all the time between reason and emotion. But this kind of rationality (so elementary that it only just deserves the name) differs, as much as chalk from cheese, from the kind of rationality which Bertrand Russell was looking for and failing to find: the kind of rationality which would ensure that our world was ordered by reason – or, to put it more exactly, that the legitimate desires of all human beings were conditioned and furthered, and perhaps reconciled, by rationality. This kind of rationality is seldom seen because our desires are seldom subjected to the rational consideration which might ensure their fulfilment.

So what has real rationality ever done for us? The answer, of course, is that it has actually done a vast amount. Russell also said:

> Men fear thought as they fear nothing else on earth … Thought is subversive and revolutionary, destructive and terrible, thought is merciless to privilege, established institutions and comfortable habits; thought is anarchic and lawless, indifferent to authority, careless of the well-tried wisdom of the ages … Thought is … the light of the world, and the chief glory of man.

What he says here does not contradict his comment quoted earlier, because this kind of thought – or rather, the desire to pursue this kind of thought – is rare indeed. But it has done great things for us, and can do still greater things if our emotions incline us to set it in motion and to pursue its course assiduously, without let or hindrance.

This kind of untrammelled rationality is the means by which our civilisation develops and improves. All progress subverts existing wisdom. That is why it is so slow and so hesitant. When women claimed the right to vote, their campaign was motivated by emotion, and opposed by the emotions of others, but it succeeded because, in the end, there was no rational case against it.

It is also true that this untrammelled rationality is necessary, and we have it to thank, for the whole vast realm of science (built upon creative thought but always subjected to rational analysis and criticism). Without rational thought, and the resolve to pursue it wherever it leads, science could not exist – although its emotional underpinning sometimes pokes through the surface when scientists falsify their results through a desire for fame or a dislike of the conclusions to which rationality seems to be leading.

Logic, too, is something that is wholly dependant on rational thought and could not exist without it. As an example of pure rationality, I think of *Principia Mathematica*, the book in which Bertrand Russell and A.N. Whitehead set out to reduce mathematics to logic, taking over 350 pages to prove that $1+1=2$ and going on to produce three massive volumes. Russell said it took so much out of him that he was never quite the same again. Whether anyone has read the book from cover to cover I do not know: certainly the publisher had misgivings about its saleability because Russell and Whitehead were required to pay part of the cost of publication. But although the book is indeed a work of pure rationality, it was certainly not motivated by rationality. Its authors embarked on the project because they *wanted* to: they had an emotional desire that they needed to satisfy in this way. And Russell is on record as saying that they "got stuck" for at least one long period, and they must sometimes have experienced a desire to give up which was overcome by a stronger desire to continue. But evidently they never had a desire to apply anything but rationality to the work itself.

One reason for the rarity of rationality is that it has a number of enemies. First among them is the fact that so many people are simply not equipped with any ability to be rational (beyond the kind of everyday ability described in the story about the Chinese and Indian restaurants, and even that may sometimes be absent), or any desire to be rational, or any understanding of rationality. Most people just aren't much good at it, and surely no one at all is so good at it that they can pursue it infallibly to incontestable conclusions. The ability to think rationally is not, as it is sometimes supposed to be, a sort of universal possession. It exists on a sliding scale and depends on education, experience, knowledge and (class) intelligence. Somewhere at the top of the scale is the kind of ability that gave rise to *Principia Mathematica*. Up there with it, or indeed above it, is the kind of ability possessed by great scientists. Down some way below that is the ability needed to succeed in an intellectually demanding profession. But there is still a long way to go until we reach the bottom, where we find many people who, through no fault of theirs, simply do not engage with real rationality at all. Bernard Shaw came up with some percentages:

> Two per cent of the people think. Three per cent think they think. And ninety-five per cent would rather die than think.

On that basis, non-thinking would characterise ninety-eight per cent of the electorate, and it is with them that politicians must ingratiate themselves. There may be a little bit of exaggeration here, but not a lot. Narcissistic charlatans have been elected to positions of power on both sides of the Atlantic because people have applied no rational thought to their posturings. Conspiracy theories catch on and proliferate because many people have an unthinking fondness for rather astonishing things – such as the idea that President Trump was waging a secret war against the Satan-worshipping and cannibalistic paedophiles who rule the world, or that Hilary Clinton and other Democrats were connected to a child sex ring run from the basement of a Washington pizzeria called Comet Ping Pong (which is a real restaurant but has no basement) – and no desire at all to evaluate them by means of rationality. This is politics as entertainment.

Russell, by the way, came to much the same conclusion, and expressed it much the same words, as Shaw:

Many people would sooner die than think. In fact, they do.

Another enemy is one which, though it goes largely unnoticed, seems to me important. You could call it *labelling* – labelling designed to exclude rational consideration, and in particular rational argument, doing so by building the conclusion into the premise. It is, in a way, a begging of the question, but that phrase is so much misused today as to have lost the subtle and useful meaning (enshrined in the latin *petitio principii*) that it used to have. Some examples are needed. Someone who refers to "red tape" is referring to rules which they want you to accept as a pointless inconvenience, but which probably amount in fact to desirable safeguards. (More red tape might have prevented the financial crisis of

2008 and saved the lives of the 72 people who died in the Grenfell Tower fire.) A politician who refers to the "nanny state" probably wants to dismiss without discussion any suggestion that some disadvantaged citizens need help to meliorate their disadvantages; and one who speaks of "throwing money at the problem", so conjuring up an image of the ridiculous, probably knows full well that solving the problem would involve expense and so is anxious not to solve it.

Someone who speaks of a "loophole" in the law wants you to believe without thought that, through some oversight on the part of those who framed it, the law fails to say something that it obviously ought to say but which, in all probability, it would actually be wrong for it to say. Someone who talks of a legal "technicality" is referring to a rule which they wish you to see as a needless obstacle to the doing of justice, but which may in reality be necessary to ensure that justice is done. (When Colin Stagg was acquitted of the murder of Rachel Nickell, his acquittal was said to be "on a technicality", the police reinforced this by saying that they were not looking for anyone else, and he was vilified accordingly; but in fact the murder was done by Robert Napper, who later confessed to it and went to Broadmoor). In all these instances something is given an immediate prejudicial description which is designed to pre-empt any rational discussion of its real nature and possible merits.

This kind of labelling is applied also to people, and applied in such a way that, if you accept it, you do not look behind the label. So common is this device that two *Times* journalists provided examples of it while I was struggling with this chapter. In one case "a class of 14-year-olds arrived for their music lesson [at a girls' school] in miniskirts and skimpy tops" and the music teacher joked that they had "more flesh on display than a meat market". Some of the girls were outraged and circulated a petition to have him fired. If the story ended here, there might be a genuine issue for rational consideration: does a remark like that justify dismissal? But according to the journalist the teacher was "popular and extrovert", he had supporters who would have defended him but for "fear of being bullied", and the girls who complained were "entitled" and "self-righteous".

In the other example, the journalist went into a bookshop and said how nice it would be when the plastic anti-Covid screen protecting the cashier was removed. Here there could be another genuine issue for rational discussion: should these screens be removed or might their continued existence be justified? But the "wuss behind the till" subjected the journalist to "a gibbering tirade of entitlement … about how much safer he felt with a 'barrier' in place, and how if they ever removed this protection from his horrible germy customers he wouldn't be able to do the job."

These two cases raise a genuine issue on both sides of which there is room for rational argument. (More so in the second case than in the first, as it seems to me.) In both cases, however, one side of the argument – the side which the journalist disfavoured – was attributed to people who were described in such a way as to scorn and dismiss them. In one case it was attributed to girls who were bullies, entitled and self-righteous. In the other it was attributed to a gibbering wuss who let loose a tirade of entitlement and referred to horrible germy customers. (It is hard to believe that he really used that phrase, so there may be some journalistic licence here.) If you take these descriptions on board without thinking, as you are meant to, then that side of the case falls by the wayside, for who would endorse an argument put forward by people like these?

If, contrary to expectations, you do apply rationality to

some of these descriptions, they turn out to be meaningless. The concept of entitlement is used pejoratively by both journalists, but what is the entitlement to which the people in question are not entitled? Are people not entitled to express their feelings? If they are, then entitlement surely resides more in the journalists than in their victims. Other pejorative descriptions designed to invalidate the views of people to whom they are applied are "do-gooder" (usually an insult aimed at someone who wishes to do good by someone who has no desire that good should be done) and "self-appointed" (a description that would fit Albert Einstein as he put forward his theory of relativity while working as a clerk in the Swiss patent office). A really killing description is that of a "self-appointed do-gooder" (which would fit William Wilberforce as he campaigned against slavery).

I have an irresistible urge to quote two other examples of labelling, taken from later editions of the same newspaper. In one a journalist, speaking of Benjamin Netanyahu (at a time before the war between Israel and Hamas), described a wide range of people who disliked his "robust leadership", including "those whose anti-Zionist voices dominate the United Nations, the European Parliament and the BBC", as reacting to him with "pearl-clutching horror". Although it is just possible that one or two of these people wore pearls, it is safe to assume that none clutched them in horror, but the attempt, successful or not, to label them as ridiculous is obvious enough. In the other example, a *Times* leader writer launched a violent attack on the charity A*mnesty* for criticising a policy of the Ukrainian government. He referred to the charity's defence of its criticism and said, not that this defence was issued, or made, or offered, or announced, or published, or put forward, but that it was "ululated".

More could be said about this particular enemy of

rationality, but let's move on. Another and equally important enemy is *rationalisation*. Its purpose is to put a gloss of rationality (which may or may not be wholly spurious) on an act or opinion which is in fact dictated by pure emotion – emotion that is pure in the sense of being unalloyed, but not necessarily in the sense of having any moral purity. Rationalisation seems originally to have been a psychoanalytic term, coined in 1908 by Dr. Ernest Jones, one of Freud's early followers. He described it as "the inventing of a reason for an attitude or action the motive for which is not recognised". It is now a term in common use, and one that has perhaps acquired a rather wider meaning. Jones's definition assumes that the real motive in an unconscious one: very likely it is, but it may also be conscious. Rationalisation, in the sense in which I use the term here, encompasses all attempts to convince oneself, or to convince other people, that one's acts or opinions, although not formed through any process of reasoning but rather dictated by conscious or unconscious emotion, are nonetheless rationally justified.

The American senator, Ted Cruz, provided an example of rationalisation, again while I was writing this chapter. Speaking about the latest of a long line of school shootings, this time by a young man with a semi-automatic rifle at Uvalde, he said that if you could eliminate all firearms from America, not only would that particular massacre still have occurred, but there would be substantially more murders than there currently are. That's the rationalisation. What it seeks to rationalise is his emotional wish that Americans should not be denied their guns or their ability to acquire guns. Or perhaps that is not his own wish: perhaps his wish is only to pander to the people who have that wish. Be that as it may, the rationalisation marks itself as a rationalisation by its very absurdity.

As a lawyer, I should like to think that UK court judgments are, in applying the law to the facts, examples of pure rationality, but of course they are not. The appeal system is enough by itself to dispel that idea. If pure and perfect rationality prevailed throughout the judicial system, a judgment would never be reversed by an appeal court. I like to think that, when a lower court makes a "wrong" decision, this is only because the lower court has a marginally poorer grasp of the law or of pure rationality – that only seldom is it wrong because emotional bias on the part of judges or magistrates has been concealed by rationalisation. I am not sure that this is quite as true of decisions of the UK Supreme Court. If a case reaches the Supreme Court, this is usually because there is some uncertainty about the law, and inevitably the Justices are inclined to resolve the uncertainty in the way in which they would like to see it resolved. This opens the door to rationalisation. In his book, *Playing off the Roof*, the former Supreme Court Justice, the late Lord Brown of Eaton-under-Haywood, explained why he approved the second application of Jonathan Sumption QC to be appointed straight from the Bar to the Supreme Court:

> I was sufficiently troubled by what I had begun to regard as the excessive soft-heartedness (I almost wrote woolly-mindedness) of a number of my colleagues, particularly in any case supposedly raising human rights concerns, that I felt an injection into the court of some stern intellectual rigour and legal conservatism had become essential.

Here he assumes his own rationality and that of Lord Sumption (as Jonathan Sumption did indeed become), but levels a rather strong and unexpected accusation of rationalisation against other Supreme Court Justices. Similarly, Lord Hope of Craighead, in the third volume of his *Diaries*, says that one of his fellow Justices "looks at apparent and misconceived paradoxes which might be corrected" and has in consequence an "ability to fix on the wrong point".

Despite such occasional departures from strict rationality, there is nothing in our legal system to justify the apparently quite common belief that judges are there to decide cases according to their own whims, rather than according to pre-existing laws not of their own making. When the *Daily Mail*, criticising a decision about Brexit by Divisional Court judges, appeared with its notorious headline, "Enemies of the People", it seemed at first sight that those responsible for the headline must harbour this wholly false belief. But perhaps they themselves knew better, and aimed the headline at readers who did not.

Mention of the UK Supreme Court tempts me to hark back for a moment in order to give a remarkable example of the way in which ignorance, even in high places, impedes rationality. In his book, *In the Thick of It: The Private Diaries of a Minister*, Sir Alan Duncan refers to the five week prorogation of Parliament which took place in 2019 at the behest of Boris Johnson. This was declared unlawful and void by the Supreme Court. Duncan describes its President, Lady Hale, as "rather batty", and later records Sir Iain Duncan Smith saying that the Supreme Court Justices "are all lecturers and are of a quality far below that of proper experienced judges." Duncan himself adds, "For once I agree with him." But the fact is that all the eleven Justices who joined in this decision had been "proper experienced judges" and had been elevated to the Supreme Court precisely because they had distinguished themselves in that role. The Supreme Court is a not unimportant feature of the constitution, but neither of these supposedly rather distinguished parliamentarians knew the first thing about it.

In the United States Supreme Court the belief that judges decide cases according to their own desires would be very much closer to the truth. That court has a quite different function from ours and there, I would make bold to say, rationalisation is rife. How else to explain the desire of American Presidents to appoint Justices to the Supreme Court whose political views are known to correspond with their own? President Eisenhower appointed Earl Warren and William Brennan, who both turned out, to his regret, to be rather liberal Justices. In 1958 someone asked him if he had ever made any mistakes, and he replied, "Yes, two. And they are both sitting on the Supreme Court." (Eisenhower invited Earl Warren to a White House dinner, took him aside and tried to persuade him not to support the desegregation of schools, doing so in words that could probably not be printed in this book. It was an appalling thing to do: Warren ignored him, and the Court ruled unanimously in favour of desegregation.)

When the Supreme Court Justices seek to interpret the American Constitution, they look at it through spectacles coloured by their own emotional political vision. In June 2022, the court reversed its earlier decision about abortion in *Roe* v. *Wade*. A naïve watcher might think that both decisions were inspired by a simple wish to interpret the constitution objectively and correctly, and that one lot of Justices did it better than the other lot. But if that simple wish were always the Justices' motivation, Presidents would gain nothing by choosing Justices according to their political views. The fact is that, when *Roe* v *Wade* was reversed, the majority of the present Court did not see in the Fourteenth Amendment what the majority of the previous Court had seen and what the minority of the present court still saw. And the reason why the majority did not see it was simply that they are more conservative now than the majority was then. Of course the present majority advanced reasons for their decision, just as their predecessors had done for theirs, but the reasons of one lot, or both lots, were necessarily rationalisations. The Fourteenth Amendment itself stands unchanged and still says nothing explicitly about abortion: it is the political persuasions of most, but not all, of the Justices that have changed.

The present majority of the Justices are not just conservative but radically (some might say recklessly) so. This is because three vacancies occurred during the presidency of Donald Trump and he appointed strongly conservative Justices to fill them. (He is on record as claiming for himself the credit, if such it is, for the reversal of *Roe* v *Wade,* and just for once he spoke the truth.) The liberal Justice, Ruth Bader Ginsburg, had tried to hold her cancer at bay just long enough to prevent Trump from replacing her during his term, but she failed. In her book, *Nine Black Robes: Inside the Supreme Court's Drive to the Right and its Historic Consequences,* Joan Biskupic describes the result:

> The Court had no middle, no center to hold. Conservatives were galvanised by their number. And Donald Trump, who had demonstrated so little respect for the law, truth, and democracy, had changed the balance for at least a generation.

Whether or not Biscupic had it in mind, her first sentence is a clear echo of Yeats' *The Second Coming*:

> Things fall apart; the centre cannot hold;
> Mere anarchy is loosed upon the world.

It might be just a little unfair to compare Trump himself to Yeats' "rough beast, its hour come round at last, [slouching] its way toward Bethlehem to be born".

One of Freud's friends was a Swiss pastor called Pfister. He applied psychoanalytical insights rather strikingly by saying, "Tell me what you find in your bible, and I will tell you what kind of person you are." Surely he was right; and if you substitute the US Constitution for the bible, this aphorism could well be applied to the American Supreme Court Justices. It could of course be equally well reversed: "Tell me what kind of person you are, and I will tell you what you find in the Constitution." Or in the bible.

However much we may try to pretend otherwise, rationality is always subject to our emotions, is always initiated by our emotions and may always be diverted, stopped or rejected by our emotions. It's unavoidably in the nature of the human race that this is so. But the world would be a better place if we could conceive an emotional desire to temper the expression of our emotions with a stronger dose of rational interrogation. And it's that thought, I suppose, that underlies most of the chapters still to come.

I cherish the story of the philosopher A.J. Ayer (later Sir Frederick Ayer) who, on being introduced to his future wife, described himself as a logician, only to find that she had misheard him and took him for a magician. I do not know how long it took for this misunderstanding to be resolved.

THREE

Conscience

There is thought to be something, if not exactly sacred, then at least sacrosanct, about the conscience. Albert Einstein said:

> Never do anything against conscience even if the state demands it.

To much the same effect is the advice of Walt Disney's Jiminy Cricket to Pinocchio: that if in danger of yielding to temptation, he should give a little whistle, and always let his conscience be his guide. And the very same injunction is to be found in a song of Marvin Gaye:

> Oh, darling, my darling, oh, yeah
> Let your conscience be your guide.

This elevation of conscience to the supreme commander and arbiter of human behaviour – a voice that should go unquestioned and should always be obeyed – requires some justification, and there is little to be had.

What we call the conscience is a loose collection of judgments, impulses, feelings and prohibitions that are supposed to promote behaviour which is thought to be moral or "good". But of course popular ideas about what is or isn't good are changing all the time. When I was a young man, homosexual behaviour was generally thought to be bad, and sending men to prison for it was thought to be good. Few people had any conscientious objection to that. Nowadays anyone who condemns homosexual behaviour is thought to be bad – homophobic is the word for it – and those who welcome gay marriage are usually thought to be good. (This at least is so in our own part of the world: in other places, gay men are blindfolded and thrown off high buildings, executed in other ways, flogged in sports stadiums, or merely imprisoned, and this, too, is thought to be an expression of morality. While I was writing this book, Uganda made homosexual conduct a capital offence.) And, as I have pointed out elsewhere, it seems likely that a member of a tribe of head-hunters would have suffered from a guilty conscience if he failed to join his fellows on a head-hunting expedition.

Hard though this reality may be for humankind to bear, the fact is that such changes and variations of conscientious attitudes must call into question the respect with which we treat the conscience and its promptings. The fact is that our consciences, like all the other aspects of our personalities, are simply the result of the diverse factors that have gone into the making of us. We are certainly not born with consciences, let alone with the same consciences. "The conscience embodies the rules and standards learned as children". That sentence expresses an obvious truth, but it happens to be borrowed from a recent article by a psychoanalyst, and it brings to mind the psychoanalytic idea that we are born uncivilised and that, if we are to become civilised ourselves, each one of us must replicate the process – a difficult and unwelcome process – through which humankind has had to pass in order to become civilised. (Well, to become as civilised as we have so far managed to be: Mahatma Gandhi, when asked what he thought of Western civilisation, said he thought it would be a very good idea.)

Whether or not it is true that each one of us, if we are to become civilised, must replicate the civilising process, the fact certainly is that our individual consciences vary one from another just as do the sources – parents, teachers, peers and others – from which they are derived. We do not manufacture our own consciences, and the sources from which some people derive theirs are, to put it mildly, not up to the job. If you are brought up in a law-abiding neighbourhood by good, loving and understanding parents, you are not likely to have the same sort of conscience as someone whose upbringing, if it is worthy of the name at all, is in a gang-ridden area and by a parent who is a dedicated criminal, addicted to drugs, anger and cruelty. In the latter case you yourself may well grow up with a conscience that does not condemn cruelty, crime, anger or drugs and, because of this deficiency, you may find yourself emulating your parent and then you may find yourself in gaol. Or you may not: other influences just might help you to turn against the influence of this parent and live a good life. In neither case, however, will your conscience be self-created. And in both cases, it will be grounded in emotion and may owe little to rationality.

The Newgate Calendar was a popular collection of supposedly true stories about crime and criminals which began to appear in the mid-eighteenth century. My own much later edition includes the story of Sawney Beane, who was born "sometime in the reign of Queen Elizabeth". He married "a woman as viciously inclined as himself" and

> they had a great number of children and grandchildren, whom they brought up after their own manner, without notions of humanity or civil society. They ... supported

themselves wholly by robbing; being, moreover, so very cruel, that they never robbed anyone whom they did not murder.

Or murder anyone whose body they did not subsequently eat. The Beanes, who lived by themselves in a cave where "legs, arms, thighs, hands and feet of men, women and children were hung up in rows, like dried beef", were eventually found and apprehended, together with their then forty-six children and grandchildren, "all begotten in incest" (though only the grandchildren, surely) and

> they were all executed without due process, it being thought needless to try creatures who were even professed enemies to mankind.

I certainly don't guarantee the truth of this story, but I tell it because the authors of *The Newgate Calendar* clearly endorsed this outcome and its readers probably did so too. Brought up in isolation as they were, the Beanes' children and grandchildren had no chance of forming a conscience that forbade them to do what the family were doing, and they cannot have avoided becoming, like their parents, "enemies to mankind" – but it was thought right to execute them for being what they were, even though they had no chance of being anything else.

Even today, of course, the lack of a "normal" conscience will not exempt you from, or reduce, your penalty if you commit a crime. And in America, believe it or not, it can actually increase your penalty from imprisonment to execution. In 2023, Brent Brewer, a 53-year-old man, was executed in Texas by lethal injection, watched by the family of his victim whom he had killed in the course of a robbery when he was 19. In Texas, a prerequisite for a death sentence is a jury finding that the accused is likely to commit further acts of criminal violence. A psychiatrist who had never clapped eyes on Brewer testified nonetheless that he was indeed likely to do so because he "had no conscience". And that diagnosis, absurd or not, put an end to him.

To say what he said in the quote that starts this chapter, Einstein must have thought that he himself had a strong conscience and that he could rely on its goodness. He may well have been right. But if he intended his aphorism as an instruction to people at large, as seems to be so, he must have supposed that everyone's conscience was of the same quality and nature as he thought his own to be. And there he was rather surprisingly, but quite obviously, wrong. Surely Shakespeare was wrong, too, when he caused Hamlet to say that "conscience does make cowards of us all" and equally wrong when, in the same play, he gave these words to Polonius:

This above all: to thine own self be true,
And it must follow, as the night the day,
Thou canst not then be false to any man.

In both cases there is an assumption that everyone is in possession of a "normal" conscience. Sadly, the upbringing of many people is such that their consciences affect them hardly at all, let alone make cowards of them, and most serial killers could claim that, as they go about their work, they are being true to themselves.

But this belief that we all have some sort of "standard issue" conscience, which we choose either to obey or to ignore, is still widespread. A few years ago, a lady approached me about a revolutionary idea which her father had conceived and which, after his death, she wanted to promulgate. Their idea was that the way to abolish all crime would be to abolish all criminal penalties. She and her father believed that it was the threat of punishment that permitted and encouraged people to commit crime because punishment, or the risk of punishment, took away the feelings of guilt for their crimes which criminals would otherwise have suffered, so assuaging their consciences and allowing their criminality to flourish. If, on the other hand, they knew for certain that they would not be punished under any circumstances, their consciences would come into full force and stop them in their tracks. She was as implacable in her belief that this would happen as I was in mine that it would not. We parted on fairly good terms, although she did liken me to a horse that could be led to the water but not made to drink.

The fact that the conscience is neither inborn nor standard, but wholly dependent on upbringing and other influences, explains why people were admired in the past despite behaving in a way that we should now condemn. Statues commemorate the lives of people who, despite the good deeds they may have done, were heavily involved in the slave trade. Of course there is a case for removing these statues. Statues are erected to people to whom we are expected to look up (in both senses) and no doubt it is inappropriate to look up to people like these. But we surely cannot blame them for what they did: through their parents and others, they absorbed the values of their time and acted on them. There seems sometimes to be an unspoken belief that they should nonetheless have rejected those values: they must surely have *seen* that slavery was wrong, the argument goes, and so they deserve to be vilified. But that would assume, once again and quite wrongly, the existence of some sort of timeless standard conscience. There are aspects of our present day values, incorporated in most people's present day consciences, which I hope our descendants will condemn as strongly as we today condemn the acceptance of slavery. Will they vilify us retrospectively for accepting the moral principles that prevailed in our time but have been rejected in theirs? Not if they are a little more rational than we are.

In the past, the conscience has been tied to religious belief and sometimes it still is. Perhaps that is why it is accorded a degree of respect which is really unwarranted (that and the fact that it is mistakenly supposed to be almost synonymous with "goodness", and you have to respect goodness). Long ago, when I was a young solicitor, I worked in firm with two partners. The senior one was a calm and quiet man who specialised in conveyancing. The other was primarily a litigator who combined irascibility with a strong Christian faith. One day for some reason I laid claim to having a conscience but confessed that I had no religious belief. This second partner was genuinely perplexed and said, "But what use is your conscience to you then?" Some people might ask the same question now, but very few: religious belief may of course play a part in shaping the conscience (not necessarily for what I would call the better), but the conscience is not nullified by the lack of it.

I did not stay long in this firm, largely because of the return of Mr G, the managing clerk. He had been away for some time because of an illness from which he had now recovered. He had lost weight and occasionally he would pull aside the top of his trousers (necessarily held up by braces) to demonstrate the large gap which existed between his body and their circumference. His other habit was to say, every so often and quite cheerfully, that he had been married for thirty years to the wrong woman. Very gradually he re-established his position within the firm and diverted to himself much of the work that I was supposed to be doing. I could write a book about my legal life, but it is not this book.

Later on I got to know Leo Abse, the Labour Member of Parliament for Pontypool, later for Torfaen, and also a solicitor. He was a campaigner for causes – including the legalisation of homosexual behaviour, the abolition of capital punishment and the reform of divorce law – all of which I supported. He managed to agree with the then Bishop of Exeter the basis for the Divorce Reform Act 1969. The provisions of this Act have been condemned in recent times and have now been superseded by changes which allow "no fault divorce", but people forget that the 1969 Act was, in its day, a liberalising measure and a great improvement on the previous law. There was indeed a lot of opposition to the 1969 reforms from those who thought them too liberal, and at Abse's request I wrote some articles in support of the changes. And then he asked me to help him write an autobiographical book to be called *Private Member*, a title he chose because of its faint overtones of *double entendre*. I really wanted to do it, but he disliked my efforts (rightly so, I think) and we, too, parted company – but not before he had begged me several times to "cultivate an elastic conscience". He implied that he had managed to do so himself. (He sought other help with the book, which was later published. I did get a brief acknowledgement.) As the Iraq war was looming, he wrote to *The Times* suggesting a way in which it might be avoided: "Assassinate Saddam", he said. The assassination of heads of state might indeed prevent wars, or bring them to an end, so saving thousands upon thousands of lives, but other heads of state are reluctant, for obvious reasons, to endorse this strategy.

I am old enough to have lived through the years of the Attlee government, and I remember Attlee saying that the conscience "should be a still, small voice". I think he made this comment to Professor Harold Laski, whose conscience prompted him to offer frequent criticism of government policy and to whom Attlee also said, "A period of silence on your part would be appreciated".

Since conscience varies so much from one person to another, is there any way, however hypothetical, of standardising it – of deciding how it would ideally be constituted? What is the morality that it "ought" to embody and uphold? Unless you want to answer this question on the basis of religious doctrine (which doesn't actually provide any satisfactory answer anyway), the only basis for morality must surely lie in some ultimate and unchanging "target" that can be generally accepted – a universally agreed conception of the way things ought to be or become. But what might this be? One answer that comes to mind is "the greatest happiness of the greatest number", but of course that answer is wholly inadequate. What about minorities? What about the animal kingdom? What is happiness anyway, and is the attainment of happiness really the thing that matters most to us: do we want something like Aldous Huxley's *Brave New World,* a world of simple undisturbed contentment (a state produced by the officially-sanctioned use of a drug called Soma)? Huxley wrote his deeply pessimistic book as a riposte to H.G. Wells, whose optimism about the future benefits of science to the human race he did not share.

And in any case, could we be sure that our present-day judgements about all these things would be endorsed by our descendants (if they had the chance to decide)? As all these questions pile up, it is plain to see that no agreed and permanent target could possibly be devised. If it could, and if after that we could go on to decide and agree upon the kind of behaviour that would conduce to our eventually hitting it, then and only then we might arrive at a fixed system of morality. But the second part of this two-stage process is, if anything, more problematic than the first and the whole endeavour would be doomed to utter failure. In the meantime we have to put up with an unreliable and fluctuating system of morality that has no firm or lasting basis and changes from person to person and from time to time.

One thing at least emerges from all this. Our present consciences cannot be relied upon to promote any general conception of morality (whatever that may temporarily be) and morality itself is not on any account to be equated with kindness.

If evidence of this rather obvious point were needed, I think we should find it in the current disagreements about LGBTQ+ and gender dysphoria. There's a difference of opinion between two groups of people. The first group asserts that someone who is born a man can transition so as to become in every possible sense a woman, and *vice versa*. The second group asserts that, although someone who transitions should be recognised as having done so and treated with complete respect, they have not in reality changed their biological sex. Those in both groups are so constituted as to take the views they take, there is no reason to think them dishonest, and an outsider might see their differences as involving mere matters of definition, perhaps even as matters to be resolved, if they can be resolved, by lexicographers. But no: those in the first group seem to be led by their consciences in different directions. They are led, on the one hand, to have the utmost concern – a moral concern, surely – for those who transition, and, on the other, to think it morally right to condemn those in the second group, subjecting them to a degree of sustained hatred and bullying that drives them out of their jobs or changes their lives in other ways for the worse. So here we have a situation in which the same consciences, driven apparently by the same impulses, promote kindness on the one hand and cruelty on the other. The "woke" agenda seems often to feature little modern castles of ultra-kindness kept in place by buttresses of longstanding savagery.

Speaking of savagery, look for a moment at criminal responsibility which is imposed, in the United Kingdom, on children from the age of ten. No other countries in Europe, and very few in the whole world, impose criminal responsibility at so low an age – an age at which the part of the brain associated with the acceptance of moral values has not fully developed and won't do so till after adolescence. It is said to be justified because ten-year-old children should be expected to "know right from wrong". This test of knowing right from wrong surfaces elsewhere in the criminal law, but what does it mean? It cannot entail merely the knowledge that two categories, so labelled, are generally supposed to exist. That knowledge by itself can surely form no foundation for criminal responsibility. The test must entail also a knowledge of what actually goes into the two categories – of the things that are "wrong" and the things that are "right". I myself do not have this knowledge and neither, I venture to say, does anyone else. Of course some things are obvious, aren't they? Killing people is wrong … unless, of course, you are fighting a war against them, and your war is a just war, and you're not violating the Geneva Convention, in which case you may get a medal rather than a prison sentence. And helping people is right … unless your help allows them to continue a life of crime, or it deprives your own family of its needs. But to these supposedly obvious things there must be added things that are not at all obvious, and things that change categories from one time to another. I always thought it was wrong to punish homosexual behaviour, but my view has only recently become right. I think now that it is wrong for criminal responsibility to start at the age of ten, and I hope to become right at some future time even though I am no longer alive to see it happen.

But what, you may wonder, has all this talk about knowing right from wrong got to do with conscience? The answer is, very little, and that's the point. All this *knowledge* – knowledge of facts, knowledge of current attitudes, knowledge of this, that and the other thing – is totally irrelevant as an actual predictor of good or bad behaviour. What matters is not whether a child, or anyone else, *knows* the difference between right and wrong (whatever exactly right and wrong are currently thought be), but whether or not their individual conscience *propels* them in the direction of the wrong or the right. Anyone may have the fullest knowledge of all the things that are considered to be wrong, but still delight in doing them because they have not acquired a conscience that stands in the way. If you're accused of a piece of bad behaviour, it's no good saying, however truthfully, "My conscience is clear", and expecting to be exonerated.

In saying this, however, and in saying one or two other things in this chapter, I may be stepping too soon into subjects treated in later chapters, so let's move on. Just before doing so, I should like to make a complaint about my own conscience which, I suspect, may be echoed by other people about theirs. Mine did not at the time inhibit me from behaving in ways that it now condemns. This kind of delayed guilt – guilt in hindsight, guilt generated, I suppose, by increased knowledge and understanding – is a very painful and unconstructive feature of a strange and fallible aspect of the human personality.

T.S. Eliot has put in no appearance in this chapter yet, but some words of his may be relevant here. In *The Cocktail*

Party, he has the psychiatrist, Sir Henry Harcourt Reilly, say to Edward Chamberlayne:

> Your business is not to clear your conscience
> But to learn how to bear the burdens on your conscience.

FOUR

Altruism

This is going to be a mercifully short chapter because it's really an offshoot from the previous one.

My own dictionary defines altruism as "respect for others as a guiding principle of action; unselfishness". Another definition speaks of "disinterested and selfless concern for the wellbeing of others". So selflessness is intrinsic to the idea of altruism: by definition, altruists gain nothing for themselves from their altruistic acts. No one, I think, would seriously contest this, but it certainly isn't true. There is no such thing as an unselfish act and, if altruism really depends on unselfishness, then there's no such thing as altruism. This is another a little bit of reality which we don't care to bear.

There's some interesting stuff here. It's widely recognised that there are indeed some people whose altruism is only apparent (narcissistic altruists, they're sometimes called) and who really do gain something from it for themselves: recognition. They want to be seen as good people doing good things, and so to attract credit and praise. They do good to others only so as to be seen to do so. I recall a rich American socialite, being interviewed on television, who was surprised and affronted when the interviewer appeared to be ignorant of her many charitable contributions, on which she then dwelt. But these people – so received wisdom has it – are something of an aberration and must be clearly distinguished from genuine altruists who seek no such kudos and really are selfless to the core. Except, of course, that they aren't.

Don't imagine for a moment that I'm trying to devalue what we call altruism: I'm all in favour of good being done, no matter what the motives are for doing it. All I'm trying to do is to make the really rather obvious point that all altruists do good *because they want to*. No one has ever decided to be altruistic for no reason at all. No one has ever manufactured their own altruism. Altruists are so constituted that their good deeds give them emotional satisfaction and that's why they do them. The good things they do make them feel good about themselves, and they would feel bad about themselves if they didn't do any good things. Just as consciences in general vary from person to person because they result from the differing influences brought to bear upon them, so also does altruism, or its lack.

Ernest Hemingway had it to much the same effect in *Death in the Afternoon*:

> I only know that what is moral is what you feel good after and what is immoral is what you feel bad after.

FIVE

Savagery

In 1963, an exhibit was added to others in the Bronx Zoo. Labelled as "The Most Dangerous Animal in the World", it proved to be a mirror in which the human visitors to the zoo could see themselves reflected. Many years earlier, Friedrich Nietzsche had said:

Man is the cruellest animal.

No one who has given this assertion a moment's thought can doubt its truth. Humankind is still most certainly a savage species. Perhaps the savagery was necessary for us to reach our position at the top of the evolutionary tree, but it does not seem to have diminished all that much since then. We have, with our invented weapons, established mastery over nearly all the other life forms on the planet, no matter how much bigger and stronger they may be. It is only the really small life forms, the microbes, from which we have anything still to fear. It was the microbes that destroyed the alien invaders in H.G. Wells's *The War of the Worlds*, and in the end it may be the microbes, through pandemics, that destroy our own species too.

But what concerns me here is another piece of reality that humankind cannot bear to recognise: the extent and ubiquity of our savagery, not towards other species (although there's plenty of that), but towards our own. One of the most remarkable things about humankind, surely, is something on which few people remark: our endemic cruelty to one another. We have no strong inhibitions against killing or wounding members of our own species, or inflicting upon them harm of many other kinds, in many different ways, physical, material and psychological. The fact that all this harm is done by ordinary people to other ordinary people is obvious enough, but we tend to put it to the back of our minds and attribute it to the evil propensities of some human beings who bear no resemblance to us, rather than to an underlying savagery which is common to our species as a whole. Freud was surely right to reject this idea:

> Civilised society is perpetually menaced with disintegration through [the] primary hostility of men towards one another.

You could say that if everyone had some sort of an ideal conscience, it would prevent all this cruelty, and in theory perhaps it would. But that is not the root of the problem. The simple fact is that, for whatever reason, we are by nature savage creatures and that our fellow creatures are not exempt from our savagery: if that were not so, there would be nothing for conscience to prevent. The extent of our savagery is of course mitigated by the kindness and concern with which we usually treat those close to us and by the benevolent and charitable institutions which our society has established, including in particular those intended, if not always effective, to prevent people from falling into destitution, to preserve or restore their health, and to save them from lawlessness and crime.

None of this is in doubt. But nor is there room for doubt about our habitual savagery to one another. You need only to pick up a newspaper to have it confirmed – confirmed mainly by the news reports, of course, but also by the journalism, because some journalists trade in cruelty. The range of savagery is vast: the killing, maiming and bereavement inherent in the waging of war; the hurt that results from the thousands of financial scams practised every day; the homophobia, racism and antisemitism that still infects so many; the modern slavery that still exists; the vicious internet trolling designed to cause pain; the cruelty to children which includes sexual abuse and bullying, the slamming shut of their growing minds, the damning up of their emotions and the sapping of their confidence; the delayed and inadequate treatment of the mentally ill and mentally disabled and their physical and psychological abuse by carers. No one goes through life undamaged by their fellow human beings.

Oscar Wilde, sent to prison for doing things that it is now legal to do, wrote in *The Ballad of Reading Gaol*:

> This too I know – and wise it were
> If each could know the same –
> That every prison that men build
> Is built with bricks of shame.
> And bound with bars lest Christ should see
> How men their brothers maim.

Wilde was writing specifically about the harm done by imprisonment, and perhaps this verse would sit more aptly in one of the chapters about crime still to come, but I like to see it as saying something of more general application.

And few things please us more than to find a hate figure, someone whom it is by common consent right to treat with wholehearted condemnation, a scapegoat for our own sinful savagery. We really do love to hate. Very often the popular press will find a hate figure for us, but suitable candidates for the role are apt to change over time. Years ago, the favoured targets of John Gordon, writing each week in the *Sunday Express*, were homosexuals – "so vile a man", I remember him calling one of them. Nowadays a different kind of vileness must be attributed to a different kind of scapegoat. But whoever he or she may be, the behaviour of the hate figure must never be the subject of any kind of understanding.

Understanding and savagery cannot easily co-exist. Irrationality and savagery, on the other hand, can always do so. The irrationality of the anti-vax movement, for example, has involved a lot of savagery. In August 2022 Lisa-Marie Kellermayr, an Austrian doctor who had encouraged her patients to have the coronavirus vaccine, was driven to suicide by the hatred and violence to which anti-vaxers had subjected her and from which the police, writing her off as an attention-seeker, had failed to protect her.

It is important to recognise our savagery for what it is: a fundamental component of the human constitution. It isn't just an exaggerated form of bad behaviour in which bad people indulge for bad reasons. It is a part of us. To my mind, it brings us back to the idea that each of us, as we grow up, must pass, if we are to become civilised, through the civilising process. William Golding, in his *Lord of the Flies*, sets out to show what happens over a long period to children stranded alone on an island who have not completed this process or, having just completed it, regress for want of its reinforcement. (A film was made of Golding's book, its credibility impaired a little by the perfect haircuts which the boys retained throughout the action.) Regression to the thoughtless savagery of childhood must surely account for much of the violence in the adult world. If we complete the civilising process successfully then our savagery will be at least modified. We shall probably not become habitual criminals, although we shall probably not see anything wrong with a great deal of "accepted" savagery, precisely because it *is* accepted. Not long ago it was accepted that criminal punishments should include hanging, beheading, drawing and quartering, crushing, boiling to death, breaking on the wheel and burning at the stake. Savage though these punishments unarguably were, they were generally endorsed.

The old time punishments just described are of course equalled and exceeded by modern day punishments inflicted in other parts of the world. In recent times, Isis has cut off the heads of its captives, roasted them over fires, drowned them in cages and lowered them into tubs of acid. It has also hooded homosexuals and thrown them from high buildings, sold nine-year-olds into slavery and, on at least one occasion, burned to death a caged prisoner to the applause of children. (If the children really did applaud, and were not forced to do so, there is some slight reinforcement here for the idea that we are all born savage.) No matter what ideology may be associated with these punishments, they cannot be necessary to uphold it: they are devised by people who simply revel in the unbearable suffering of others.

If you have the bad luck to be born a Dalit in India, your life will be hardly worth living. Dalits are India's lowest caste, considered "untouchable". Despite some legislation, their presence and touch are still thought by other castes to be poisonous, and they are often the victims of harassment, violence and even murder. Any definition of the word "savagery" would certainly embrace this kind of behaviour towards the Dalits, but those who indulge in it, or sanction it, would not recognise it as such. To them, presumably, it is simply an accepted and acceptable aspect of the world in which they live. They express in this way the savagery that lies within them without noticing that they are doing so, let alone feeling any sense of guilt about it.

And the same is true of the rest of us as we go about our everyday lives, giving vent unconsciously to our own savagery in many different ways. Take, as a small example, the case of a constituent of the Labour MP, Luciana Berger. She had been the victim of grossly antisemitic behaviour and, when interviewed, the constituent condemned this behaviour in the strongest terms. He said it was totally wrong and unacceptable that she should have been treated in this way, and then he spoilt it all by adding, "even if she is a Jew". This is an interesting example of a common phenomenon. The constituent would have thought of himself as a good man with a good conscience saying good things. He may even have thought that he was a still better man for defending someone who was inherently ... well, a little bit like a Dalit because she was a Jew. The idea that it is absolutely wrong to stigmatise Jews in any way, and that there is no reason, let alone justification, for doing so, must simply have passed him by because he had been raised to *see* them as stigmatised. This paragraph was written before the tide of antisemitism was let loose by the Israeli-Hamas war against Jews who had nothing whatever to do with it. Although there is controversy, the better view seems to be that T.S. Eliot, too, harboured antisemitic views. I mention this only because I see no other way to bring him into this chapter.

Two instances of this phenomenon of disparagement figure in my own experience. When I was a consultant in a firm of solicitors in Westminster, one of my colleagues made a rather laboured comment about the food to be provided at a function hosted in barristers' chambers to which we had been invited, pointing out that some of the people there would be unable to eat some kinds of food because they were Jewish, but that there would therefore be "all the more for us". It took me a long time to realise that he said this in order to convey, without ostensibly doing so, the fact that he himself was not a Jew. As if I cared. Some years earlier I was working for a legal publisher and confided in a senior colleague that I had been invited to join the staff of the Law Commission. He looked at a list of the lawyers already working there, referred to one who had an obviously Asian name, and said, "They're scraping the bottom of the barrel there, aren't they?" And both these colleagues of mine had seemed to me among the nicest people I had ever met.

Consciously or unconsciously most of us are always looking for ways to express our savagery. And although some people just let theirs fly without compunction – internet trolls, for example – most people prefer to find a way of doing it which is generally sanctioned or approved, so that they need suffer no inhibitions before they do it and no guilt afterwards. That's why cruelty to the Dalits caught on and still persists. It's also, surely, why right-wing populism seems attractive to many people: it overrides rationality and conscience but, if we embrace it, we can think of ourselves merely as subscribers to a recognised ideology. And it's why we insist on the retributory punishment of criminals instead of trying to eradicate the causes of crime ... but don't start quarrelling with me about that now because I've more to say about it later on.

The world is not made up of two classes of people, different in kind, the good guys and the bad guys, let alone of the people who have consciously chosen to be good and those who have consciously chosen to be bad. People do not, by and large, even see themselves as good or bad, and have certainly not deliberately chosen to be either. It is simply (to use a biblical quote) that time and chance happeneth to them all. Luciana Berger's constituent simply didn't realise that he was being cruel in stigmatising her as a Jew (cruel not only to her if she heard him, but to any other Jews who heard him). He was just reflecting the world as he had been taught to see it.

Sometimes, however, those who express their savagery realise full well that they are doing so but are untroubled by it, seeing it as somehow acceptable or justifiable. Acceptability is illustrated by a case reported while I was writing this chapter. Four robbers, using a sledgehammer, broke into the home of a retired footballer. In front of his partner and his young children and armed with a knife, they grabbed him by the neck and threatened to cut off his fingers with a set of pliers. He said that the look of terror on the children's faces would never leave him. This is a fairly average example of the savagery employed by violent criminals. It's a fair guess that these offenders recognised that their behaviour was savage (or recognised at least that it could be described as savage) but accepted it as a useful means to their end.

Supposed justifiability is illustrated by the doings of Isis, described above. It is of course illustrated also by war. Unimaginable suffering is unleashed by wars often fought for reasons that are supposed by both sides to be "good". The fact that we have yet to agree on any reliable way, other than war, to settle the differences between nations, or upon any way to prevent aggressive wars such as the war in Ukraine, must surely point to the fact that, as a species, we don't care *quite enough* about this suffering. Imagine, if you can, visitors from another planet, their spacecraft just close enough to earth for them to see, with their telescopes, the ant-like groups of *homo sapiens* trying to destroy one another, and watching this with a sort of detached incredulity, asking themselves what the hell (if hell is a concept of theirs) is *wrong* with this species?

When Sir Tony Blair (as he then wasn't) was asked to choose a favourite song, he came up with *The Green Fields of France* (otherwise *No Man's Land*), written by the singer-songwriter Eric Bogle about a young soldier who died in World War I and whom he named Willie McBride:

> For the sorrow, the suffering, the glory, the pain
> The killing and dying were all done in vain
> For young Willie McBride it all happened again
> And again, and again, and again, and again.

This was before Tony Blair embarked with George W. Bush on the Iraq war.

On a scale smaller than war, savagery is expressed in everyday revenge, vengeance, retribution … call it what you will. The cruelty involved in this is nearly always thought to be justified. It is encapsulated in the exhortation, adopted by President John Kennedy, "Don't get mad, get even." If you have been cruel to me, I am justified in being cruel to you. Or, to put it more generally, if you have been cruel to someone, then cruelty is due to you.

In an earlier book, I recorded the reported reactions of American citizens to some botched executions that had taken place there. Lethal injections had left the offenders to variously choke, struggle and writhe in apparent agony for periods of between half an hour and two hours. Speaking of one or other of these cases, the citizens said:

> "What that guy got, he deserved", "Who cares if he feels pain?", "Serves that piece of crap right … hope it was painful for him", "Cosmic justice, a horrible end to the life of a horrible man" and "Why should we give him a humane death when he didn't give his victim a humane death?"

You may think these comments to be justified. Personally I don't, but that's not why I mention them: I am seeking merely to point to the savagery that they undoubtedly express. If we were not a savage species, we should still have to apprehend and deal with anyone who committed a murder (on this hypothesis, an unlikely event) but we should not be saying things like this.

Those states of America that still retain capital punishment (27 in number at the time of writing, although five have declared a moratorium over its use) are finding it increasingly difficult to carry out. They can no longer obtain some of the poisons they want to use in their lethal injections. Sometimes the medically-untrained executioners can't even find a vein to take the injections. Sometimes other methods, such as gassing, don't work. Hence the botching and the agony. Has it occurred to anyone but me to wonder why they don't give the prisoner the option of drinking the lethal drink that allows people so quickly, efficiently and infallibly to take their own lives in Zurich and elsewhere? Is it because this simple solution would be somehow too lenient, allowing the prisoner to die by their own hand rather than by the cruel and fumbling but implacable hand of the state?

There is of course another category of savagery which may overlap with those mentioned earlier but which is a little different: savagery which is practised by people simply because they derive active and conscious enjoyment from the practice of savagery – enjoy the infliction of pain and other kinds of suffering – because time and chance has made them sadists. Sadism has to do more with power than with sexuality, though its practice may give sexual satisfaction, and it ranges from the grossest physical torture to the infliction of everyday humiliation. (I once overheard a shop manager saying contemptuously to an assistant that he was "useless".

I had the strong impression that he was accustomed to issue this insult, and that the assistant, who looked rather as a beaten dog might look, was accustomed to suffer it.)

What about empathy? Why does empathy not stand in the way of our savagery? What we have to say about empathy is surely much the same as what we have to say about the conscience (and it can be argued that empathy achieves nothing unless it is allied to conscience): that it is a feature of the personality which we possess in unequal measure and which some of us do not possess at all. Even if we do possess it, it tends not to extend to the "others" – to those with whom we do not identify, to anyone who is not "one of us", to anyone not a member of our tribe. In Nazi Germany, the Jews were the others, viewed as a sub-human species on whom suffering could be inflicted because their suffering didn't matter (and was often relished). Another example is provided by the Bosnian war, in which a hundred thousand Bosnian Muslims were slaughtered by Serbians, just because the Bosnian Muslims were not the Serbians. And to the members of Isis who did the deeds described above, "the Kafir's blood is halal for you, so shed it". The chapters in this book are meant to have some relation to one another: the chapter on perception is still to come, but it is already obvious that our savagery towards the others is usually based upon – and is let loose by – a misperception of their nature.

In the Brexit referendum, I voted remain for one reason only: that the long term survival of the human race seemed to me to depend on its disparate groups coming increasingly together, staying together, and not splitting apart. Amongst all the arguments expressed in the lead-up to the referendum, I never heard this one made, and I thought that sad and significant. The truth surely is that the more we see different countries, groups or groupings as the "others", the more room there is in the world for hostility. Whatever the eventual results of Brexit may be, this at least seems to be already apparent.

Is it possible to imagine a world peopled by human beings to whom it is simply unthinkable, inconceivable, unimaginable to inflict suffering on members of the their own species? Might evolution ever produce such human beings? Perhaps not, but how completely our world would be transformed if that were ever to happen. Our whole lives would be changed, changed utterly. And to imagine the extent of this change is to see very clearly the extent of our present-day savagery.

Meanwhile we shrug aside the words of Antonio Gueterres, the Secretary-General of the United Nations. Speaking in August 2022 and referring to what is perhaps the ultimate embodiment of our savagery so far, nuclear weapons, he said:

> Today, humanity is just one misunderstanding, one miscalculation away from nuclear annihilation. We have been extraordinarily lucky so far. But luck is not a strategy. Nor is it a shield from geopolitical tensions boiling over into nuclear conflict.

Is it not astonishing that we do not find this astonishing? Perhaps our remote descendants will find it astonishing. Assuming, of course, that there are any.

I daresay that few people these days read the work of Patrick Campbell, the Irish humorous writer who, on his father's death, became Lord Glenavy. I used to enjoy his articles and stories enormously. He had a stammer, as I did (although mine, in its day, was worse than his), and he wrote about it in a way that made me laugh out loud. I allowed him to portray the funny side of it because he knew what it was really like. People who don't know what it's really like but make fun of it nonetheless are just displaying their casual savagery. (This still happens, for instance in films such as *A Fish Called Wanda* and *Inkheart*, and in books like Andrew O'Hagan's *Mayflies*, in which he gives a gratuitous stammer to a pet shop owner. In 2008 the journal *Speaking Out* carried an article by a stammerer who happened also to be blind and who said, "Blindness is much easier to live with than stammering".) Patrick Campbell wrote beautifully, and he attributed his writing skill to the advice of Robert Smyllie, the editor of the *Irish Times* for which Campbell wrote at the start of his career:

> A sentence must flow as smoothly as milk from the Great Tit of the Shuddering Sacred Cow of Cahirciveen. Milk it, Mr Campbell, sir. Milk.

It would surely be difficult, by the way, to think of better general advice than this to give a writer and I myself try hard to follow it, not with unmixed success. But the point of this digression is not really to talk about stammering, nor yet about writing, but rather to refer to an early story of Campbell's about a radio programme which featured a character to whom he refers as Mum, in conversation with Wilfred Pickles, whom people as old as me will remember mainly as a radio quiz master. I quote:

> "Tell us, love," says Wilfred, "just before you go – what do you think about things in general – what do you think … sort of … about everything."

> Mum doesn't hesitate. Not for a single second … "Well, Wilfred," she says, "I think if … everyone was nice to … everyone else the world would be … nicer."

"And very nice, too," says Wilfred.

Campbell riffs for some time on the absurdity and banality of this answer and on the time, trouble and expense involved in conveying it the listening public. An accompanying drawing by Ronald Searle shows him reaching into his radio set in order to strangle Mum.

A recent newspaper article set out to show that no racial group is more savage than any other, and that may be true. The heading was, "There's no such thing as a warlike race". But there is such a thing as a warlike species, and that's us.

SIX

Religion

Much of humankind – not all, but very much – cannot bear the reality from which religious belief shields us: that there is no God, that our lives have no purpose beyond themselves, and that there is no other world for us to live in when we die. T.S. Eliot himself wouldn't have classed this among the unbearable realities he spoke of because he didn't think it was a reality. He was a Unitarian who converted to Anglo-Catholicism in 1927. Earlier he wrote *The Hippopotamus*, a poem in which the Church is compared to the beast of the title. In the end the hippopotamus goes to heaven where "he shall be seen performing on a harp of gold". Furthermore:

> He shall be washed as white as snow,
> By all the martyr'd virgins kist,
> While the True Church remains below
> Wrapt in the old miasmal mist.

Religious belief is of course a belief in the supernatural. One expression of it, or justification for it, is embodied in a Latin phrase with a history so long that there is doubt about who first said it:

Credo quia absurdum

It translates as, "I believe because it is absurd". It stands beside another such phrase, "*Credo quia impossibile*", of which no further translation is needed. So much has been written in recent times about religious belief that originality is hard to come by. If faith in religion means enough to you – if you have been told about God by people you trust, and it brings you comfort to believe in him – you will see your world through God-coloured spectacles and your faith will probably prevail against all odds. But for those who are not in this position, belief in God falls apart in so many ways, and in so many places, that there is simply no greater absurdity.

But so what? According to the Latin tag, it is its very absurdity that makes religion true. It was not so long ago that that those who questioned religious faith were called "rationalists". Rationalists were people who applied rational thought to religion, and this was considered an eccentric and peculiar thing to do. It was a sort of category error: religion was a fundamental truth impervious to enquiry. Our puny reasoning might make it look absurd, but so much the worse for our puny reasoning. Its very essence resides in the fact that it is above reason, and *this is the fact* that makes it true. Gradually, at least in the case of Western religions, things have changed. With the development of science, we have come increasingly to see rational thought as competing on equal terms with religion, and indeed as superior to it, at least in the sense that religion must be somehow reconciled with rationality if it is to be worthy of belief.

At the heart of the problem is the supposed nature of God. To religious people, God is by definition the creator of everything. At my kindergarten we started each day by singing:

All things bright and beautiful
All creatures great and small

All things wise and wonderful
The Lord God made them all.

And to a religious believer the Lord God made not only those things, but also the very universe itself and the very laws of nature. He alone created gravity, the concept of space-time, quantum mechanics (at present comprehensible only to him), the double helix of DNA, the second law of thermodynamics and the first one. He alone knows whether dark matter really exists, whether string theory is true and whether T.S. Eliot was right to say that the world ends not with a bang but with a whimper. He alone ensured that nothing could travel faster than the speed of light, that $E=MC^2$, that fire was hot and ice was cold, that two and two made four, and that life existed on a tiny planet that circled the sun in the unimaginable vastness of space and that a few of its life forms had what we call consciousness and fewer still had some capacity for rational thought. And he could – really could and really might – have done it all quite differently.

We could of course wish that, in many respects, he *had* done it differently. Sam Harris has pointed out, in *Letter to a Christian Nation*, that having the urethra going through the middle of the prostate is a clear design flaw in men. God might have refrained from creating motor neurone disease, dementia, depression, cancer and parasitic worms ... the list could go on and on. He might not have created a world "where youth grows pale, and spectre-thin, and dies". He might have given everyone a merciful death and not subjected so many to a prolonged and undignified one, dominated by pain and distress. And what about this?: he could surely have spared us the tedium of having to urinate and defecate. How? I've no idea, but an omnipotent God could, by definition, have done it.

If it be the case, as it seems to me, that people have created God, rather than God them, they have certainly done their best to create him in such a way as to make his existence impervious to question. It's no use trying to question it by invoking natural laws and employing our own rationality because God is by definition the creator of these things and so is throned above them. He is in every possible sense super-natural – above all nature, including us. So nothing that I say is likely to shake the faith of someone with religious belief. If you look inside yourself and find God there, that's probably enough for you. But ... well, if there is a God, he is the creator of such rationality as we possess and I feel an urge to apply mine as best I can. If our rationality is God-given, it a strange thing that, if we do apply it, it seems to point so clearly to his non-existence.

I have never put this to the test, but I have often imagined myself about to begin a discussion with a religious believer and making, before we start, a prediction which I commit to paper but do not disclose. It goes something like this: "Within ten minutes you will be telling me that my questions cannot be answered because we cannot fathom the ways of God." This might be called the "unfathomability" response. To my imaginary believer, a response of this kind would seem perfectly reasonable, but it is also the response which he or she would have to make if there simply were no God. It is exactly the same response that I should have to make to questions if I were to start a religion based on the existence of fairies. ("They created everything. They can perform miracles. They've done wonderful things for me. I know you can't see them or smell them or touch them or hear them, but that's the whole point: you must have *faith* in them. And if you do they will give you eternal life.") If you start with a premise that leads to questions that are of their nature unanswerable, it may be that your premise is wrong.

Reason would suggest that, if there is a God, he is more cruel than loving. If all the suffering that exists in God's world at any given moment were to be concentrated into a single agony for a single person, it would kill them stone dead in a split second – mercifully. But the suffering is in fact distributed among the millions of people who experience it every day and whose suffering is relieved by no mercy. How is this to be reconciled with the existence of a loving God? A believer might respond that humankind brings all this suffering upon itself, but that would be manifestly untrue (and even if it were true, it would invite the question: why would a loving God create a species that did that?). Or he or she might respond by saying that it is all part of God's plan, but what plan could it possibly be that God – an omnipotent God, mind you – can bring to fruition only in this way? Or he or she might respond that God simply does not intervene in his creation, but if that were so there would be no point in prayer – and in any case his creation itself might justly be called cack-handed.

Religious believers certainly behave as if God does intervene in his creation, but they do so rather strangely. To take a typical example, *The Sunday Times* reported on 6 December 2015 that the conviction of Oscar Pistorius for killing Reeva Steenkamp had been upgraded on appeal from manslaughter to murder. The victim's mother said that this was a "success … due to the justice system and God." In attributing this result to God, she had no thought of blaming him for the original verdict, or indeed for allowing her daughter to be killed. On 4 September 2014, *The Times* reported that, because of DNA evidence, Henry McCollum had been freed from prison in North Carolina, where he had spent decades on death row after convictions for rape and murder. He "hugged his mother and father and thanked God for his release". It did not cross his mind to blame God for his original conviction or for his decades on death row. Closer to home, I received recently a Christmas message from a husband and wife which referred to the wife's longstanding treatment for cancer: "God has given her more good days than bad, so we continue to give thanks for His grace". Not for the world would I point this out to them, but there is an obvious illogic in holding God responsible for the good days, but not for the bad ones or for the cancer itself. For most religious believers, their religion is so deeply entrenched that such contradictions bounce away without even entering their consciousness. God's goodness must somehow be preserved. Christine King Farris was the sister of Martin Luther King. Her life was shot through with tragedy: she had to suffer his assassination, the drowning of her other brother and the shooting of her mother as she played the organ in Ebenezer church. She soldiered on, living to 95, saying, "God never puts on us what we can't bear". Perhaps she hadn't noticed that people kill themselves because of what they can't bear, as my son did. Certainly it didn't occur to her to wonder why God had required her to bear so much.

Reason suggests also that God is more incompetent than omnipotent. Evangelists explained the Indonesian tsunami in 2004 as God's punishment for sexual immorality in tourist nightclubs, the flood in New Orleans in 2005 as God's judgment on a sinful city and the earthquake in Haiti in 2010 as the result of a "pact with the devil" which Haitians had apparently made over 200 years before. All these disasters caused a vast amount of suffering, but they completely missed the target because most or all of the suffering was inflicted on people who had nothing whatever to do with the sins supposed to have precipitated them. Reasonable believers, anxious to avoid association with this sort of nonsense, might write off these evangelists as the nutcases that they clearly are, but instances of gross unfairness are to be found in the bible itself. Deuteronomy 5.9 quotes God as saying that "I thy God am a jealous God, visiting the iniquity of the fathers upon the children unto the third and fourth generation ...", and Numbers 14.18 has the same quote. And when Naaman is cured of his leprosy and Gehazi runs after him to swindle him out of money, Gehazi is told that the leprosy of Naaman will cleave not only unto him, but unto his seed for ever (II Kings 5.27). For *ever*. To be fair, however, these biblical examples are perhaps of casual cruelty rather than incompetence.

But surely there is another instance of incompetence that is much less easily dismissed. When Charles Darwin pipped Alfred Russel Wallace to the post by publishing *On The Origin of Species*, Christians saw it as a threat to their religion, as of course it was. (Darwin's wife was distressed because she thought that Darwin would not now be joining her in heaven.) The idea that our species has evolved from apes was hard to square with the idea that God has created us in his own image. But religion adapts to threats, and in due course most Christians came to believe that, although God's true purpose had indeed been to create our own human species, he had done so by means of evolution – the evolution which, of course, he himself created along with everything else. (Why he should have chosen to do it in this way was necessarily another instance of unfathomability.) So far so good; but how to explain all the evolutionary false starts? Evolution produced many human species (fourteen according to one count), and relegated them all to extinction, before it hit God's supposed target and produced *homo sapiens.* And if to create *homo sapiens* was God's intention all along, as Christians believe, his timing looks inexplicable. It seems likely that the Big Bang occurred some 13.8 billion years ago, the earth was formed some 4.5 billion years ago, and life began on this tiny planet some 3.5 billion years ago, but nearly all of that last 3.5 billion years was to pass before *homo sapiens* began even to exist, a mere 200,000 years ago. The old hymn tells us that a thousand ages in God's sight are like an evening gone ("short as the watch that ends the night before the rising sun"), but this seems ridiculous – or rather, unfathomable.

Evolution is of course a very gradual process. The time it took us to evolve from our ape ancestors to being the people we are today may be short in cosmic terms, but it is very long in human terms. At what point along this journey did we cease to be the animals who had no expectation of an afterlife and become the animals who could look forward to one? Was there a first inhabitant of heaven – a heaven empty save for him or her and unlikely to be very enjoyable?

Reason prompts the question, why does God not make his existence known? (Bishop Desmond Tutu said, "We know God is in charge: we just wish He would make it more evident sometimes.") The earth is full of people worshipping Gods of different kinds and different dispositions, or worshipping no Gods at all, or wondering whether there are any Gods to worship. In an essay called *Memorial Service*, the great American journalist H.L. Mencken set out the names of 185 gods, adding: "They were gods of the highest standing and dignity – gods of civilised peoples – worshipped and believed in by millions. All were theoretically omnipotent, omniscient and immortal. And all of them are dead." If only our God – if it's our God that exists – would demonstrate his existence in such a way that everyone would see and accept it, would that not be of incalculable advantage to the whole human race? Christians would claim that God's failure to reveal himself is a part of his plan because "salvation comes through faith", and it is faith for which God will reward us. This again is surely another answer they would have to give if God did not exist, but even on its own terms it makes little sense. If we are so constituted as to lack faith, this is not our fault and there is nothing we can do to generate it.

Another reasonable question is, why did God create us at all? Some might say that he did so in order to confer a benefit upon us, but that would be nonsense. Before our creation, we did not exist, and no benefit can be conferred upon an entity that doesn't exist. Could he have done it because he wanted to fill his heaven with good people, and his hell with bad ones? Surely not. No omnipotent God, with that simple end in view, would need to go through all the billions of years of hit-and-miss palaver that I have tried to describe, creating in the end an imperfect species prone to disease, disability and premature death, as well as to internecine cruelty and warfare. No, this may be the most unfathomable question of all.

Let's end this attempt at rationality, appropriately enough, with some more questions about the afterlife. When Robert Runcie, the former Archbishop of Canterbury, was dying, he is reported to have told his family about some of the people he was going to meet in heaven. St. Augustine was the only one that I remember. He was expressing the Christian view of the afterlife – an existence in which we, recognisable as ourselves, would meet the people who had died before us (and, in the course of "time", those who died after us), recognisable as themselves. This existence would never, ever, end and our happiness would be everlasting. What a wealth of unfathomable questions this raises. Alan Clark, the womanising memoirist and Tory MP, son of Lord Clark of Civilisation, asked another Archbishop of Canterbury, Geoffrey Fisher, whether there would be dogs in heaven. Fisher said certainly not. Clark was very upset. Should we laugh or cry?

The fact that those in heaven must do without dogs would surely be the least of their problems. Life here on earth consists in change and striving. We are born, we grow up, we bury or cremate our parents, we marry or acquire partners, we have children, we rear them, we watch their progress, we earn money by working, perhaps we delight in our grandchildren, we retire from work, and if we are lucky we enjoy our retirement before we die. Most of us do all these things; all of us do some of them. Doing them is what gives meaning to our lives. ("Life without challenges is meaningless", as the Dalai Lama once said.) But none of us could do any of them in heaven. How are we to occupy ourselves for all eternity? What meaning or purpose can characterise an eternal life? What can it be that makes us eternally happy?

Oh, and there's another problem. When we meet our relatives, what age are they and what age are we? I was fourteen when my father died and he would not know me unless I was fourteen again, but my children and grandchildren would not know me if I was fourteen, and I should not know them if they live to a ripe old age (as I hope) and then join me in heaven in the shape of old age pensioners. Charles Causley, in a heartbreaking poem called *Eden Rock* – even as a disbeliever, I can't quote it without tears in my eyes – imagines that after death he meets his parents as they were in his childhood, still aged only 25 and 23, waiting for him with a picnic on the beach:

> They beckon to me from the other bank ... I had not thought that it would be like this.

Do we arrive in heaven healed of all our disabilities and infirmities, our physical and mental health restored? Will my residual stammer be gone, along with the deafness that has replaced it? Helen Keller, the deaf and blind American author and activist, thought she knew the answer:

> Death is no more than passing from one room to another. But there's a difference for me, you know. Because in that other room I shall be able to see.

And Baby Peter and all the other babies and young children who die prematurely, perhaps brutally at the hands of their parents or carers: do they reach heaven and remain as babies and children, presumably healed of their illnesses and injuries and mental scars, or do they grow up? And how are they or any of us to be happy if we are to be reunited and to live eternally with those who made us unhappy on earth? Are we to be separated from them, or do they change, or do we change? The unfathomability response is the only one to make to all these questions.

So far I have rather assumed that our afterlife is to be spent in heaven, but what if we spend it in hell? Traditionally hell is a place of everlasting fire in which, for every moment of an existence that never ends, we feel the agony of being burnt. "Depart from me, ye cursed, into everlasting fire ..." says God, according to Matthew 25.41. Some of us here on earth express the wish that our enemies should burn in hell (though others wish that they should rot in hell – a fate that would seem incompatible with burning, but which might be almost equally unpleasant). Stop for a moment and think about this. Although some religious leaders have tried, without any evidence, to reinvent the idea of hell, characterising it rather as an unending separation from God, we still harbour this age-old idea of unending torture, and many of us still treasure the thought that others will suffer it. Yet surely it is the most terrible idea that the mind could possibly conceive: excruciating and unrelieved pain that never ends. Is this hell a thing of God's creation, in which case there can be no further doubt about his cruelty? Or is it, as I think, something that we have invented for ourselves and attributed to an invented God? Either way we seem to have accepted and endorsed it, so surely there can be no further doubt about our own cruelty.

In fact, of course, the idea of an afterlife, heavenly or hellish, comes into head-on collision with science. Everything we feel and think and know and remember – everything that makes us the human beings that we are – resides in and depends upon our brains. Cartesian dualism, the idea that our minds and our brains have an existence independent of one another, has long been recognised as false. The neurosurgeon Henry Marsh, in his book *Do No Harm: Stories of Life, Death and Brain Surgery*, describes an operation in which he inadvertently tore an artery supplying blood to the brain stem. The patient never woke up and spent the rest of his life a "grey curled-up body" unconscious in a nursing home bed. Marsh draws "the grave lesson of neuroscience – that everything we are depends on the physical integrity of our brains". And when we die, our brains rot in the grave or burn to ash in the crematorium. It would be a miracle if our personalities were to survive this. But that's no problem, says the believer: miracles are God's *forte*. Either you believe this or you don't. I don't, and I don't think I want to.

More can be said about the suffering and cruelty that is so much a part of both religion and human life. Religions tend to present themselves, not always plausibly, as pacific, but in reality they provide an outlet for human savagery: they let it rip. Without this savagery there would have been no crusades, no Inquisition. Without savagery we should have nothing to fear from radical Islamists. Without savagery, Salman Rushdie would not have been stabbed, nor his publisher shot nor his translator stabbed to death. Without savagery, there would have been no 9/11. Without savagery, the offices of *Charlie Hebdo* would not have been attacked and some of its journalists killed and injured. These things and many, many more were all done in the *name* of religion, but religion by itself did not cause them: its role was to inspire them and let loose the savagery needed to accomplish them – and to justify them in minds of those who did them and in those of their co-religionists.

Why are religious people religious? Much has been written (some of it by Freud) about humankind's wish to believe in a father-god, but it must be true that no one would adhere to a particular religion unless they had been told about it. No one spontaneously becomes a Christian or an adherent of any other faith. Some people (including Richard Dawkins) say that there should be no such thing as a Jewish child, a Christian child or a Muslim child because parents should not impose their own religious identity on children who have had no chance to evaluate it, or to choose a different one, or to choose none at all. Religious parents would disagree because, whatever their particular beliefs may be, they consider them uniquely valid and precious: why would they not make a gift of them to their children? And even if they didn't, a question mark would still hang over the idea that their reticence would enable their children to "make up their own minds" later on. We do not create our minds and we do not create the influences that bear upon them. But here, perhaps, I am getting ahead of myself: my chapters on free will are a treat still in store.

I myself have been an atheist for a long time. I went to a public school (no choice of mine, and I hated nearly every minute of it, though I still go there in my dreams) where we went to Chapel once a day and twice on Sundays. For most of my time there, the headmaster, known as "Chief", was a Canon of the Church of England. He was a stickler for sexual morality and told us, in a sermon, about an old boy who had consulted him about the sexual abstinence on which the Chief had always insisted. The old boy found himself at odds with his contemporaries who did not practise this abstinence. "These chaps seem to get on all right," he told the Chief, but the Chief would not relent. (After his retirement he became Dean of Exeter Cathedral and came to my home town one Sunday as a preacher. He told the congregation that prominent atheists, among whom he included Bertrand Russell, were atheists only because they had "run off with other people's wives".) One day at school I confided to a fellow pupil that I didn't believe in God. My choice of confidant was not a good one, because he chose to broadcast my confession widely and went on to become a Bishop. (But we did exchange Christmas cards, of rather different kinds, every year until he died some seventy years later.)

It doesn't seem to me that religious belief can survive the detached application of rationality (or of such rationality as we have), but religious believers have no emotional wish to apply it. When I was about seven years old, I was taught by Miss T, a rather Amazonian lady who told us about the Angels of Mons. These angels were supposed to have appeared in the sky, in support of the allied cause, at the battle of Mons in the First World War. The story never had very firm foundations – it appeared originally in an avowedly fictional story – but Miss T believed it implicitly. One of my schoolmates said that he did not believe it, so Miss T said that he was just a heathen.

This was a brave thing for my schoolmate to do because it was unwise to get on the wrong side of Miss T. If we annoyed her sufficiently, she would pick us up by the hair, shake us as a dog shakes a rat, and throw us sobbing to the floor. Perhaps this story belongs more suitably in the chapter on savagery, but Miss T was not a monster. And that, perhaps, is the point about savagery: savagery is usually commonplace, seldom monstrous.

Long ago I was browsing in a bookshop and came across a book of memoirs called *On The Look-Out* by C.H. Sisson. I had never heard of Sisson, as probably I should have done, but I picked it up and did something I should not have done: I looked at the ending:

> Before my window the fields stretch away to the Dorset hills; the willows, no longer pollarded, have not all been removed. The river flows or overflows among them, according to the season. What it all means, God knows.

I bought the book because this passage appealed to me, but I had completely misunderstood it. I had read it as a sort of throwaway shrugging of the shoulders, the reference to God not to be taken literally but used simply as a confession of baffled incomprehension, an assertion of meaninglessness (as one might say, in answer to an awkward question, "God alone knows"). But not at all: Sisson was a deeply religious man. He meant exactly what he said. To him, God really did know what it all meant. And he wanted to end his book by saying so. Sisson died in 2003 and perhaps he will by now have acquired this knowledge for himself. But I don't think so.

When the poet Shelley died in 1822, the journal, *The Courier*, said:

Shelley, the writer of some infidel poetry, has been drowned. Now he knows whether there is a God or no.

Well, maybe so and maybe not. Even today the idea persists that you will discover, after death, whether or not God exists. If he does exist, you'll certainly discover that, but if he doesn't exist you will discover nothing. Only a miracle can keep you conscious after death: if no God, then no miracle and no consciousness. No one's going to be disappointed.

SEVEN

Death

There is something about the reality of death, and the implications of it, which humankind is unwilling to bear. The something is the fact that the dead do not exist – a fact that is obvious but often belied by what we say and do. The implications are … well, we'll come to them. Mark Twain will crop up later in this book as one of the "celebrity" disbelievers in free will, but I want to quote him here on the subject of death:

> I do not fear death. I had been dead for billions and billions of years before I was born, and had not suffered the slightest inconvenience from it.

We can infer that he did not expect his death to usher him into heaven or hell, and from here onwards I too shall discount this possibility.

Mark Twain's quote is interesting in several ways. He may be quite truthful when he says that he doesn't fear death but, whatever our beliefs may be, most people do fear it and always have done. For my part I increasingly echo the Latin phrase, originally of religious origin and much quoted in medieval writings, *Timor mortis conturbat me* – fear of death disturbs me. Of course, what we're talking about here is not fear of the process of dying, which may be prolonged, painful, distressing and disorientating, but rather the fear of death itself – the fear of being dead. Philip Larkin expressed it perfectly in *Aubade*:

> The sure extinction that we travel to
> And shall be lost in always. Not to be here,
> Not to be anywhere,
> And soon; nothing more terrible, nothing more true.

Larkin said that the greatest trick of humankind, thought to be the only species on earth that knows it's going to die, was to live as if it didn't know.

Our fear of death is unsurprising, if only because evolution must necessarily have built it into us. Richard Dawkins was once asked why evolution had not reconciled us to the prospect of death. He pointed out rather tersely that this would be contrary to the purposes of evolution. There is no need to puzzle over it. Some people have argued that capital punishment is actually more merciful than life imprisonment, or at least than whole life imprisonment, because so long as convicted murderers remain alive they continue to suffer their punishment, whereas after death they are released from it and suffer nothing. But what is merciful falls to be judged by the recipient of the mercy, and very few people, given this choice, would opt for death, still less for a sudden brutal death inflicted by appointment after a period given over to the anticipation of it.

I suspect that even those who kill themselves do so despite a lingering wish to say alive. It is certainly true that, in those who try but fail to kill themselves, the wish to live often grows stronger and makes them glad to have survived. That is why we strive to prevent their deaths and are tormented when we fail. My son was a forensic clinical psychologist. Just one day before my birthday, and having sent me a birthday card that

I received the next day, he took his own life. He had suffered for a long time from the very worst of all mental illnesses: severe clinical depression, coupled with anxiety. The details are not for this book, but some days before his death he said to me, "I don't want to *die*." I emphasise the word "die" because that was how he said it – as if, to him, dying was inconceivable. I knew that he had been thinking thoughts of death, so to him it was not really inconceivable, but in some way it still was. I inferred from what he said that he had set his mind against it, but I was wrong. I was still suffering from the foolishness which had beset me throughout his illness: that his death would be so terrible that it could never actually happen. And in a strange way, it seems, he half-thought the same: I don't believe that he was ever reconciled to death. It was almost as if his illness had some motive force of its own, sufficient to overpower his wish to stay alive.

Mark Twain does something mildly surprising: he speaks of himself as being dead before he was born as well after he had died. Some might question his terminology, but in *equating* the two states he is absolutely right. The unborn do not exist, and neither do the dead. They are united in the state of non-existence.

Richard Dawkins, in a rather well-known passage from *Unweaving the Rainbow*, has surely got this wrong:

> We are going to die, and that makes us the lucky ones. Most people are never going to die because they are never going to be born. The potential people who could have been here in my place but who will in fact never see the light of day outnumber the sand grains of Arabia. Certainly those unborn ghosts include greater poets than Keats, scientists greater than Newton. We know this because the set of possible people allowed by our DNA so massively exceeds the set of actual people. In the teeth of these stupefying

odds it is you and I, in our ordinariness, that are here. We privileged few, who won the lottery of birth against all odds, how dare we whine at our inevitable return to that prior state from which the vast majority have never stirred?

It's inspirational, and of course you know what he means, but surely he is giving a sort of existence to the non-existent. The "most people" who are never going to die because they are never going to be born are not people at all. There are no unborn people. They don't outnumber the sand grains of Arabia, because there are none of them. They are not unborn ghosts. They are not a vast majority who have never stirred. We are not luckier than them, because there is no "them" for us to be luckier than. And if we whine about death, our whining is not to be dispelled by the thought that non-existent people don't exist.

I am labouring this point because humankind really does seem to have difficulty with the idea of non-existence. Death deprives us of life, doesn't it? To kill someone is to inflict the greatest harm on them that you can possibly inflict, isn't it? Murder is the most heinous of crimes? Well, yes; and yet … after death, there is no one, no entity, nothing at all to feel the deprivation or to suffer from the harm. No one has ever complained about being dead. I once read an article by a philosopher in which he solemnly went through all the experiences that living people might expect to have if they went on living, with a view to validating the idea that this is what made it wrong to kill them, but that's not the point. No one in their right mind would suggest, and I'm certainly not suggesting, that it isn't wrong to kill them. Of course it's wrong, if only because they don't want to be killed. But the strange and oddly unpalatable fact remains that people who are killed don't feel deprived of life, because they don't feel anything, because they don't exist.

The difficulty that we seem to have in accepting the fact of non-existence could be illustrated in many ways. Someone with a terminal illness was reported recently as saying, "I'm going to miss life." Sadly, she is now dead, but we can feel sure that she is not missing life. When people die, we're accustomed to say, or to inscribe on tombstones, R.I.P. or *requiescat in pace* – may they rest in peace. This phrase may sometimes have religious overtones, but it is not a specifically religious aspiration. (Those who believe in the afterlife are expecting something rather more diverting than peace.) But it assumes that the dead person might *not* rest in peace, that their peace might somehow be disturbed – "For in that sleep of death what dreams may come" was what worried Hamlet – and this could not happen unless they continued in some sense to exist. The same idea of post-death existence is illustrated in two songs that come to mind. The first is the well-known *Danny Boy*, the lyrics by an English barrister, Frederic Weatherly:

> If I am dead as dead I well may be,
> You'll come and find the place where I am lying,
> And kneel and say an Ave there for me.
> And I shall hear, though soft you tread above me.

The other is *The Unquiet Grave*, sung best by the Irish singer Luke Kelly, whose recordings survive his own death in 1984:

> I'll do as much for my true love
> As any young man may.
> I'll sit and mourn all on her grave
> A twelve months and a day.
> The twelve months and the day being gone

A voice spoke from the deep:
Who is it sits all on my grave
And will not let me sleep?

And T.S. Eliot in the *Four Quartets*:

And what the dead had no speech for, when living,
They can tell you, being dead: the communication
Of the dead is tongued with fire beyond the language of the
living.

And in May 2023 a pillar box was installed at Sedgemoor Crematorium, not far from where I live and where I shall probably go when I die, allowing people to send "Letters to Loved Ones". It followed a similar installation at Gedling Crematorium in which over a hundred letters were posted in the first few weeks. I wonder what happened to them.

Perhaps it is the idea of ghosts, and ghost stories, that illustrate most clearly "our almost-instinct almost true" (Larkin again) that death is somehow not the end of existence. This has nothing to do with religious belief in the afterlife: quite the contrary, because it has nothing to do with heaven or hell. Of course we don't really believe, do we, that the dead can return to haunt the living; that vampires can be undead, rather than really dead, and therefore able to rise from their coffins at night and suck our blood; nor, on a more mundane level, that the dead can turn in their graves if something happens after death that would have upset them in life? No, we don't really believe these things, but still our minds are not really closed to them. We don't reject them as plainly nonsensical and so unworthy of our attention.

Maybe belief in reincarnation is an example of unwillingness to accept the non-existence of the dead. Christmas Humphreys QC was a particularly effective cross-examiner who secured convictions in several murder cases at the Old Bailey (including that of Ruth Ellis, who was hanged to public outcry, and those of Timothy Evans and Derek Bentley, who were both hanged but should never have been convicted at all). He was also a Buddhist. It is said of him that, looking one morning at the obituaries in the newspaper, he remarked, "I see old so-and-so has died … again". The Buddhist belief, of course, is that our souls survive death and, until they achieve nirvana and escape the cycle of rebirth, they live again in the body, not necessarily of another human being, but perhaps of some other member of the animal kingdom. Reincarnation is quite a popular idea. You might say that you would like to be reborn as a whale, or maybe as a nightingale. But there is no sense in which the whale or the nightingale could be aware of possessing your soul. There could be no possible difference between a whale or a nightingale that has inherited your soul and a whale or a nightingale that is just a whale or a nightingale. Nor of course would you, after your death, be aware of yourself as a nightingale or a whale, so there is no sense in which you would have become one. You would have simply ceased to be.

A number of books have asked how the universe comes into being. Jim Holt, for example, wrote *Why Does the World Exist?* He finds no definitive answer. Surprisingly, perhaps, much seems to turn on the meaning and nature of the "nothingness" that is assumed to precede the existence of the universe. Lawrence Krauss, in *A Universe from Nothing*, is concerned with this same question, but still there seems to be doubt about what nothingness really is. I've got a definition if anyone wants it: nothingness is the pre-existing state of the universe as perceived by someone who is dead. Or by someone who never existed.

Death is the end of the world and it comes to many of us every day. My father died when I was fourteen. He had smoked constantly, lighting each new cigarette from the stub of the old one, and he died of a lung cancer for which he had had a radical operation, but it took him very many months to do it, marooned in bed at the top of the house. When I went back to boarding school one term, he did something I had never known him do: he wept, probably because he did not expect to see me again. But he was still alive, still in bed, when the term ended and I came back. And there he remained until one night his friend the doctor was called to put an end to him. He had books, probably a radio, certainly no TV. I used to come to his room and ask how he was. Usually he would say that he was about the same, but occasionally he would indulge me and say he might be a little better. He would mention his pain and say he hoped I would never have pain like it. One day he said, "I don't think I've been a very good father to you." I think now that he was right, but I don't think I thought so then. Certainly I didn't say so, and I'm thankful for that.

As a small boy, I often prevailed on my mother to let me buy my father packets of cigarettes, doing so at the shop called the Blue Bird, across the street from the office where he practised as a solicitor. The cigarettes I favoured, only because of the picture on the carton, were called Three Castles. There was no suggestion then that smoking was linked to cancer. I thought that I was giving him these cigarettes as acts of love, but now I see that they were rather attempts to evoke his love for me. And that they will have played a small part in killing him.

We all learn about death in different ways. I think I came across it for the first time in *The Story of Babar*, the first of the picture books about Babar the Elephant by Jean de Brunhoff

("In the Great Forest a little elephant was born. His name was Babar. His mother loved him dearly ..."). In this book there are two deaths. Babar's mother is shot by a cruel hunter hiding behind a bush, an event that I could hardly bear to see and to which I was never reconciled and, if that were not enough, the king of the elephants died, looking very green, from eating a bad mushroom – an event that did at least pave the way for Babar's own coronation.

People's attitudes to death do vary of course. Ostensibly at least, W.B. Yeats thought little of it. He chose the epitaph for his gravestone:

Cast a cold eye
On Life, on Death.
Horseman pass by.

But when he died, W.H. Auden reacted differently:

Earth receive an honoured guest:
William Yeats is laid to rest.
Let the Irish vessel lie
Emptied of its poetry.

The dead no longer exist. To borrow from the title of an Agatha Christie book, death comes as the end. But let me bring this chapter to a close on as cheerful a note as I can manage. When I was a small boy, my mother took me to an open air poetry recital. I don't think my father's interest in poetry went beyond that of Kipling and I think my mother had no interest at all, but this was something of a social occasion and that is probably why she went. One poem shook me, and I've never forgotten it. It shows how memories of the dead survive in the minds of the living. It's about Heraclitus – not the philosopher Heraclitus, but a poet who lived and died two centuries later – and it's a translation by William Johnson Cory of a tribute by Heraclitus' friend Callimacus of Cyrene:

> They told me, Heraclitus, they told me you were dead,
> They brought me bitter news to hear and bitter tears to shed.
> I wept, as I remembered, how often you and I
> Had tired the sun with talking and sent him down the sky.
>
> And now that thou art lying, my dear old Carian guest,
> A handful of grey ashes, long long ago at rest,
> Still are thy pleasant voices, thy nightingales, awake;
> For Death, he taketh all away, but them he cannot take.

The well known last line of Philip Larkin's *An Arundel Tomb* – "What will survive of us is love" – is to much the same effect, and it appears on the small brass plaque in the Garden of Rest where my wife's and my son's ashes are buried, but Larkin himself had mixed feelings about it. Andrew Motion's biography tells us that, at the end of his manuscript draft, he wrote: "Love isn't stronger than death just because statues hold hands for 600 years". This piece of truthful self-disparagement is at least preferable to the one which, according to the same source, he wrote at the end of his poem *High Windows*: "… and fucking piss".

EIGHT

Perception

Perception has to do with the ways in which we regard, apprehend, or understand things – or people, or concepts, or pretty much whatever you care to name.

One particular aspect of it has been singled out and usually called "the problem of perception". It concerns our apprehension of the outside world – the world that exists beyond ourselves. Our knowledge of this world depends on the information gathered by our senses and transmitted to our brains, and on the way in which our brains deal with it. The "problem" is that we have no way of proving that what we perceive by means of this process is an accurate picture of the outside world as it really is (or, come to that, of proving that any outside world exists at all).

No one spends much time in worrying about this problem. If you are aware of it at all, you probably assume that what seems to us to be so is what is really so. When Hamlet's mother asks him why he seems particularly upset about his father's death, he says:

"Seems", madam? Nay, it is; I know not "seems".

And of course it's true that the world as it seems must be close enough to the real world for us to live in it, apparently with reasonable success – logistical success at any rate.

Assuming our eyesight is good enough, we don't bump into the furniture because our senses haven't perceived it.

But of course Immanuel Kant was right: we cannot and do not directly know the world in itself. He saw *things in themselves* as existing in what he called the *noumenon*, to which we can never have access. (He thought that "free will" must exist in the *noumenon* because he couldn't find it anywhere else – but that, from where I'm standing, is because it doesn't exist. Much more of that later.) In *How Emotions are Made*, Lisa Feldman Barrett, an American Professor of Psychology, puts it like this (the italics being hers):

> [Y]our brain employs concepts to make the sensory signals meaningful, creating an explanation for where they came from, what they refer to in the world, and how to act on them. Your perceptions are so vivid and immediate that they compel you to believe that you experience the world *as it is*, when you actually experience a world of *your own construction*.

In *Being You*, the British neuroscientist Anil Seth says:

> The entirety of perceptual experience is a neuronal fantasy that remains yoked to the world through a continuous making and remaking of perceptual best guesses, of controlled hallucinations.

And, paradoxically, it is our brain's curtailing, interpreting and packaging of its perception of the outside world, and not any unmanageable full-on experience of it, that allows us to live in it successfully.

So much for that particular aspect of perception. Those members of humankind who understand the limitations on their power to "see" the outside world may find them a little hard to bear. But there are more unpalatable things to be found if we look at perception in its wider sense – a sense that embraces both that aspect and any other form of perceiving in which we engage.

The way in which we perceive the outside world, and particularly the way in which we perceive the other people in it, and indeed ourselves – and this is what I'm really concerned with in this chapter – depends not only on the "mechanical" workings of our senses and our brains' interpretations, but on our pre-existing feelings and attitudes. When the sensory input lands in our brains, it lands amongst the complexity of everything that is already there and is inevitably coloured by it. (A mundane example is provided by a journalist who, writing of the "pageantry" that followed the death of Queen Elizabeth, said of the heralds' tabards: "they're starting to look very silly." Silliness is obviously not a quality of the tabards themselves, but rather a quality imposed on them by the pre-existing sentiments of the journalist.)

This is something that we seldom seem to understand. When we find that our perception differs from that of someone else, both we and they may sometimes have recourse to rationality in an attempt to justify our different perceptions. And of course rationality has its place, and one of us may convince the other that our perception is "truer" than theirs. But this is by no means a foregone conclusion because the differences usually result, not from faulty reasoning, but rather from the fact that past circumstance has made us into different people with different dispositions. And it has made some of us into people who simply brook no questioning of our perceptions, who see no need to justify them rationally, and who claim very often that they amount simply to "common sense". This is the stance characteristic of the demagogue.

The ubiquity of misperception is illustrated by the fact that psychoanalysts rely upon it in order to do their job. They take care to present themselves to their patients (analysands if you'd like the technical term) as a blank screen on which the patients can project their emotional perceptions. The analysts don't say anything about their own lives, their own views or their own feelings. If they did, the screen wouldn't be blank. As the analysis proceeds, buried emotions come to the surface and are projected on to the analyst. If the patient disinters a hatred of their father, the first thing they do is to see the analyst as the bad father, and they wouldn't be able to do that if the analyst had been full of overt kindness, concern and bonhomie. This transferring of emotions is called the transference and it is the analyst's interpretations of it (and sometimes of the analyst's own reactions to it: the countertransference) that allows the patient gradually to accept the real source of the buried feelings. It has been said, with some degree of accuracy, that psychoanalysis *is* the analysis of the transference. And of course the point I'm making here is that the transference is a clear misperception of the analyst by the patient – in this case a useful misperception.

In other contexts, however, the psychological mechanism of projection is not helpful at all. Projection leads us to misperceive in other people unconscious feelings of our own that we don't want to recognise in ourselves, and we do it all the time. An unconscious feeling of resentment or hatred may lead us to "see" in someone else the characteristics that we resent or hate. The someone else will seldom be a blank screen, as psychoanalysts aim to be, and they may really have some characteristics that justify to some extent the projected feelings, but the full force of the projection comes from the person who makes it. (Both the idea of projection and that of unconscious feelings are often associated with Freud, but both are these days orthodox and generally accepted.)

Back in 1968 an article of mine appeared in a legal journal. It had nothing to do with the law. In those days the readership was less hard-nosed: the article wouldn't be published today. It had to do with four related television plays by John Hopkins called *Talking to a Stranger*. I quote from it:

> [The plays] took the events of about twenty-four hours in the lives of one family – father, mother and grown-up son and daughter – and each play showed them through the eyes of one of its members ... Yet each play was entirely different because the events of the day seemed entirely different to these four people. To the daughter, living a life of sexual promiscuity after the failure of her marriage, finding herself pregnant (she does not know by whom) and coming on a visit to her hard-faced, destructive mother and her softer, more lovable but still possessive father. To the father, his marriage disappointing ever since the painful fiasco of its first night, all his love directed at the child his daughter used to be and is no longer, escaping into his dreams of the past. To the son, who visits his parents frequently but out of a sense of duty, who has been offered promotion to a job in Australia but is reluctant to go: feeling his parents have never loved him, he seems to be restrained by his need for their love. And to the mother, whose long struggle seems to have earned her no love from any member of her family, whose bitterness is both the result and the cause of her estrangement, and who at the end of the play destroys the taut order of her life by breaking all the china and then destroys her life itself by cutting her wrists with a broken glass, revealing with her last words – "Somebody hold me" – the insecurity that has lain behind her righteousness.

The article (forgive me for quoting from it so much) goes on:

> The events of the day seemed different to all these people because they were different people and responded to the events with their different personalities. The hard-faced mother of the daughter's play was not hard-faced in her own play. The father, kindly, dreamy and misunderstood in his own play, was callous and angry in his wife's, uncaring in his son's and demanding in his daughter's ... Reality was not the same for any two of these people. It was not even the same two minutes together for any one of them.

Not long ago, I watched a television programme about Senator Joe McCarthy, who in the 1950s promoted himself as America's witchfinder-general in accusing people of being members or former members of the communist party. Perceptions of his behaviour divided the population. Many citizens revered him, and John Wayne was one. Others saw him as a lying, self-promoting demagogue, and President Eisenhower, when asked to criticise him, said, "I'm not getting down in the gutter with that guy". In more recent times, Donald Trump is similarly divisive. And in our own country, Boris Johnson divides opinion in much the same way. Why do so many of us perceive – or "see" – these people so differently? Only because the brains of those on one side of the divide are constituted differently from the brains of those on the other. Any idea that our assessments of other people (or of political systems or of almost anything else) are made by means of objective and disinterested rationality, grounded in factual knowledge, is obviously false.

C.S. Lewis got this exactly right in *The Magician's Nephew*:

What you see and what you hear depends a great deal on

where you are standing. It also depends on what sort of person you are.

Father Pfister was saying the same thing in my chapter about rationality. So no two people perceive the world in exactly the same way. The clearest example of differing perceptions is to be found in mental illness. It is obvious that the beliefs about the world that are harboured by psychotic (or "insane") patients are very different from those of most people. Some believe themselves to be gods or monarchs, others hear voices, others think themselves victims of persecution. Patients suffering, like my son, from clinical depression see the world as a dark, meaningless and hopeless place, and their own existence as an unbearable ordeal. Depressed patients may also misperceive features of the outside world: my son said of a London bus that it looked to him "distorted", and as a clinical psychologist he knew that this was a symptom of his illness. But these misperceptions are only the most obvious examples of the ways in which we all perceive differently.

There is another point to be made about perception. It has to do with *intrinsicality* – something that is very closely allied to what I called "labelling" in my chapter about rationality. It is the idea that some quality is inescapably inherent in a particular thing or idea or person. In some contexts the application of intrinsicality can't be faulted. If you say that rain is intrinsically wet, no one is likely to argue with you. But to say that something is, for example, beautiful, is to misrepresent your individual perception of it as something inherent in its nature. Beauty is indeed in the eye of the beholder and not intrinsic to anything. The same goes, of course, for ugliness. (Nowadays most of us would describe wild, bare and mountainous landscapes as beautiful, but in the past most people thought them ugly and best avoided.)

And of course it goes also for all the groups of "others" to whom we attribute the not-us-ness which fosters our dislike of them. If T.S. Eliot is to be brought somehow into this chapter it may be relevant here to attribute his antisemitism to a misperception of Jewishness.

The trouble about intrinsicality is that if something is labelled as having – or, if not overtly labelled, then just assumed to have – some intrinsic, inalienable quality, there's a strong presumption that it really does have it. There may be little or no evidence that it does, but the idea has been slipped in under the radar and this makes it hard to question. Many people would aver that the statement, "God is love", is intrinsically true. It can still be challenged, but the description discourages the would-be challenger.

If you Google "the greatest achievements of mankind", or words to that effect, you will be presented with many things purporting to answer this description. (They won't include abolishing war, or torture, or hunger, or poverty, but there you go.) And of course it's true that the human race has far, far outstripped any other life form on the planet in its cleverness, its inventiveness, its creativity, its artistry, its capacity for thought (both abstract and concrete), its science, its mathematics, its invention of reading and writing … it is a story of astonishing achievement. Isn't it? Well, is it? There is nothing *intrinsically* astonishing, or even good, about these so-called achievements – no outside criterion according to which they can be ranked as good or astonishing. Other life forms on the planet, so far as they can think at all, certainly don't think them good. It is only we who think them so. We are marking our own homework – attributing to the things we have done an intrinsic quality which they do not possess, one with which we alone have decided to endow them.

But let's come back to the most important thing that I've tried to deal with in this chapter: the way in which we so often misperceive one another and ourselves. It wouldn't be much of an exaggeration to say that this, and this alone – this and very little else – is the subject matter of this whole book. Certainly there's no chapter that doesn't concern itself with misperception in one way or another, and several of them are devoted to it. T.S. Eliot's bird, who spoke of humankind's blindness to reality, might helpfully have added that it is misperception that helps us to remain blind. Ah, you may say, but isn't it implicit in this chapter that no perception can be relied upon – that there's no *real* reality standing above, and apart from, people's differing *perceptions* of reality?

Well yes, but we mustn't go too far down that road. Some misperceptions are glaringly obvious once they are pointed out – glaringly obvious, that is, to anyone able to let go of them. No one outside India is likely to deny that the Dalits are persecuted because they are misperceived. No one who is not actually an antisemite is likely to deny that antisemitism is based on misperception of the Jews. No one who is not homophobic is likely to deny that misperception led to the criminalisation of gay men. Other examples of obvious misperception crowd into my mind and probably into yours. If misperceptions are examined carefully, their falsity really may fall away, leaving in its place something much closer to the truth. Or so it seems to me. I shouldn't be writing this book if it didn't.

NINE

Sexuality

In November 1835, two men were brought to the scaffold outside Newgate prison in front of an unusually large crowd of spectators. One of these men was John Smith. The other was James Pratt, who was also known as John and who had to be held upright because he was in a state of collapse. Apart from that, the joint hanging seems to have gone according to plan. These were the last men to be executed in Britain for homosexual behaviour.

The main factors that contributed to this event – this crazy event – have already been described: irrationality, savagery, distorted conscience, misperception and religious belief. If our hypothetical visitors from outer space had watched it with their unimaginably powerful telescopes, they would surely have sat in their spacecraft with mouths agape, silent and dumbfounded. They might well have advised other space explorers to avoid planet Earth at all costs, and this advice would be the same today because homosexual men are still being executed in other countries and in other ways.

It has been suggested that T.S. Eliot, who married twice, the first time disastrously, was gay, but this is in doubt. The poet A.E. Housman was certainly gay. He was born in 1859, only 24 years after the execution of Smith and Pratt. Homosexual behaviour, though still illegal, was no longer a capital offence but, such was the stigma still attached to it, and the constant pain of those who lived with it, that he seems to endorse self-destruction:

> Shot? So quick, so clean and ending?
> Oh that was right, lad, that was brave:
> Yours was not an ill for mending,
> 'Twas best to take it to the grave.

But at the same time, he railed bitterly against the stigma itself, knowing that homosexuality was a matter of luck, not self-creation:

> Oh who is that young sinner with the handcuffs on his wrists?
> And what has he been after that they groan and shake their fists?
> And wherefore is he wearing such a conscience-stricken air?
> Oh they're taking him to prison for the colour of his hair.

A.E. Housman died in 1936, the year I was born. During his lifetime, in 1895, Oscar Wilde had been sent to Reading Gaol for two years, and homosexual behaviour was still a crime at the time of his death. Leo Abse, already mentioned, played a large part in decriminalising it and I hope he was thanked sufficiently for that. When the tide turned, leading in the end to the possibility of homosexual marriage, Smith and Pratt were pardoned along with other men convicted of homosexual offences (much good it did them) and there is now a statue to the gay code-breaker Alan Turing in the grounds of the public school to which both he and I were sent – something that would have been inconceivable when I was there.

There are of course other forms of sexual behaviour which are still criminal, including in particular sexual acts involving minors. I don't suggest for a moment that these acts should not be crimes, but I do sometimes wonder whether they couldn't be covered simply by the laws against cruelty to children. After all, surely, it's the destructive cruelty likely to be inherent in these acts, that and nothing else, which provides a reason for criminalising them. Does the sexual nature of the cruelty justify their being singled out from all other kinds of cruelty and dealt with by special laws all of their own? Or is this special treatment just another symptom of our tendency, continuing despite the change of attitude towards homosexuality, to look on misdirected sexuality as uniquely evil, and so different in kind from other forms of destructive behaviour? Perhaps the answer is that, if such a change were made, the actual harmfulness of these acts would have to be demonstrated rather than assumed.

A better example of my point lies in the crime of bestiality, punishable originally by imprisonment for life, now by imprisonment for up to two years. If this involves cruelty, then it could surely be covered by the offence of causing unnecessary suffering to animals. If it doesn't, why punish it at all? Only because of our continuing, but unsupported, belief that deviant sexuality is somehow uniquely evil and abhorrent irrespective of any harm it may do. We punish it, certainly not because it's harmful, and not so much because we don't like to think about it as because we don't like to think of it actually happening. Once upon a time we felt the same about sodomy.

In 2023, a 25-year-old man sobbed as he pleaded guilty to the sexual penetration of a cow. He was charged also with causing unnecessary suffering to the cow, and he may have been guilty of that offence, but this seems unlikely on the face of it. Given what the cow might expect from her own kind in the way of sexual penetration, you might think that this particular experience would go almost unnoticed. However that may be, the conviction for bestiality may well have ruined this young man's life. Why – and to what purpose?

Lesbianism was never criminalised. That isn't to say that lesbians haven't been stigmatised and vilified and sometimes driven to suicide. Suicide among the whole LGBTQ+ community is more frequent than it is among other people. For some years my family and I lived in a house on the Holly Lodge Estate which backed on to Highgate Cemetery – the old part of the cemetery, not the more recent part that contains Karl Marx's tomb – and we could visit it just by climbing over the wall. In its Circle of Lebanon I found the tomb of Radclyffe Hall, the lesbian author of *The Well of Loneliness*, published in 1928, and I saw the marble plaque placed at the side by her lover Una Troubridge. On it is a quotation from Elizabeth Barratt Browning: "And if God choose I shall but love thee better after death." I could almost wish there were a God to make that choice.

But let's leave aside the sexuality I've been talking about up to now, and concentrate more generally upon what might be called "straight" sex and the heterosexual community. Nothing untoward to see here, surely – but, oh my goodness, there is. At this stage of our evolution, our attitudes even towards ordinary heterosexual sex are unnatural and contradictory to an extraordinary degree. The contradictions themselves give rise to a lot of pain, and the fact that this is so is in itself is a reality which humankind finds it hard to bear. But I think we find it harder still to accept the reality of the sheer mess we've made of it: we just take the mess for granted. Robert Boothby, the bisexual MP, later Sir Robert and later still Lord Boothby, was for a long time the lover of Harold Macmillan's wife, Lady Dorothy. Someone to whom Lady Dorothy did not seem particularly attractive asked him why, and he replied, "That's just the way it is." This is what most of us would say if taxed with humankind's strange attitude to sex.

We could begin with a quote from Woody Allen. Asked by his psychiatrist whether he thought sex was dirty, he replied:

It is if you're doing it right.

Like all the other animals on the planet, *homo sapiens* depends for its survival on the act of procreation. That statement is decorous as well as incontrovertible. But if, instead of "the act of procreation", I had said "copulation", my statement might be thought a little less decorous. And if, instead of either, I had said "fucking", the statement would have struck many people not only as indecorous but as a wilful assault on their sensibilities. And yet, strangely and paradoxically, this word – an important and significant word, you might think – is also used simply as an intensifying adjective, robbed altogether of its real meaning.

A striking example of this was provided in a television programme called *Accused: The Hampstead Paedophile Hoax*. In 2014, two children were filmed in Hampstead claiming that they and other children were being forced to engage in sexual activity by a group of local parents. It was nonsense: the children had been coached to say this by the perpetrators of a hoax that had wide and lasting repercussions. At one stage the names of the children falsely alleged to be taking part in these activities were published on the internet, together with details of their sexual proclivities. A mother of one of them, understandably incensed by this falsehood, telephoned a supposed perpetrator and said, "Get my fucking daughter's name off the internet *now*".

In 2022 a Member of Parliament was seen to be watching

pornography on his phone in the Chamber of the House of Commons. Earlier he had watched a website concerned with tractors. He was a farmer who, as a boy, had attended an agricultural boarding school just down the road from where I now live. The tractor website had apparently led him to a pornographic website, and he revisited that website on the later occasion when he was seen to be watching it. Because of this, he had to resign from Parliament. (He did so by becoming the Crown Steward and Bailiff of the Manor of Northstead, one of the two offices of profit under the Crown – the other is Steward and Bailiff of the Chiltern Hundreds – which, even today, provide the only means by which an MP can resign.)

So watching a depiction of tractors in the Commons Chamber is acceptable, but watching a depiction of sexuality is not. It is difficult to see why. I know, of course, that popular sensibilities dictate this result, but I don't know why those sensibilities exist.

The Woody Allen quote refers to the dirtiness of sex. The idea that sex is dirty – that the activity that creates our children, the activity on which the existence of humankind depends, is "dirty", even "filthy" – seems to be very firmly fixed in the minds of most of us. It's an all-pervasive idea: "dirty old man", "dirty jokes" "Dirty Digger", Richard "Dirty" Desmond, "Dirty Den", and so on. The promise of something "filthy" is often the lure of the pornographer. In February 2023 *The Times* published a report about a Roman artefact shaped as a phallus under the headline, "Veni, vidi, filthy …". And in recent times students at Oxford University set up a website called OxShag which said:

> You know exactly who it is you'd rather be doing it with in your filthiest fantasies. Our job is to bring those fantasies to life.

More recently still, an article in *The Observer* about the books of Shirley Conran, who had recently died, was headed, "Shirley Conran's legacy is not only the filthy bits, but sisterhood too".

I was certainly brought up to think of sex in just this way – as something dirty, filthy and unmentionable – by parents whose own childhoods had made them unable to speak of it. As a small boy, I asked my mother how babies fed when they were first born. She said awkwardly that milk came into the mother's arms. "*Arms*?", I said. "Yes", she said. And I was told that babies came into existence, not because the stork brought them, which was another common evasion at the time, but simply because parents wanted very much to have them. Our contorted attitudes towards sex are learned attitudes, and most of the learning comes from our parents. "They fuck you up, your Mum and Dad", as Larkin put it, again using the word in a non-literal sense, and so they do.

Freud thought that we associate sex with dirt or filth because of the proximity of the genital organs to the excretory organs. Perhaps he was right. Freud's standing seems to have declined since his death (as Darwin's has risen since his), but he was right about a lot of things. W.H. Auden's poem *In Memory of Sigmund Freud* includes a verse:

> for one who'd lived among enemies so long:
> if often he was wrong and, at times, absurd,
> to us he is no more a person
> now but a whole climate of opinion.

And even in that judgment I think "absurd" is a little harsh. Psychoanalysis is in a no-win situation: to those who haven't experienced it, its tenets do indeed seem counter-intuitive and sometimes absurd, while those who have experienced and come to understand it, are said to have been brainwashed.

Freud's interpretation may indeed be right, but it doesn't explain everything about our strange attitude to sexuality, so often perceived as shameful. We dress ourselves in clothes and describe removing them so as to produce nakedness visible to others as "indecent" or "obscene" – unless, of course the nakedness is incomplete and carefully calculated, when it may be thought desirable. It is commonplace for women to reveal their legs and arms and, particularly in evening dress, their shoulders. In the old song *The Mountains of Mourne*, the young Irishman who goes to London is asked by his girlfriend "how the fine ladies in London were dressed". He reports back:

> Well if you'll believe me, when asked to a ball
> They don't wear no tops to their dresses at all.

He was more astonished than attracted by this (he said it was difficult to tell "if they were bound for a ball or a bath") and decided that he himself would

> … wait for the wild rose that's waiting for me
> Where the mountains of Mourne sweep down to the sea.

Actresses and celebrities are particularly adept at revealing selected parts of the bodies that good fortune has given them. Breasts are not fully revealed, but there is enough revelation – usually from the top, but often from the side, sometimes from both directions, and very occasionally from below – to show that they exist and are in some sense accessible.

In my lifetime it was a criminal offence to publish sexually explicit pictures or even to write explicitly about sex. Does this negative attitude come from a fear that these things might lead to uncontrolled sexual arousal and perhaps to rape or to unwanted pregnancy – a pregnancy much more of a risk in the days before reliable contraception, and much more to be dreaded when single mothers were condemned and often deprived of their children, and the children themselves were stigmatised with extraordinary cruelty as "illegitimate" or "bastards"?

Of course our attitudes towards single mothers and towards the children of unmarried parents have changed. And so, as we've already noticed, have our attitudes to gay men and women. As a young solicitor I wrote articles for, and letters to, legal journals protesting against what was then still the criminalisation of homosexual behaviour. I was in small part inspired by my friendship with a young gay medical student whom I had known since school, and who was being treated for what was called his "inversion" by a Jungian analytical psychologist – not "psychoanalyst" because psychoanalysts are Freudians (or Kleinians). I don't think he had much luck with that. (He told me one day that a nurse had approached him spontaneously and given him what he described as a lovely kiss. Perhaps it is sad that this gesture can have led to nothing more for either of them.) My protests didn't go down well. One editor refused to publish them. And a fellow solicitor accused me publicly of *nostalgie de la boue* (perhaps best translated as a hankering for dirt). On reflection, it may have been gay men, not me, at whom this gibe was levelled – or perhaps it was levelled at both them and me. And yet today gay people can actually be married to one another in the eyes of the law, if not in those of the Church. This particular change may have been encouraged by the realisation that homosexuality is, as Housman was surely saying, determined, not chosen – a realisation that might one day extend to criminality in general (more of that to come).

Other important changes have happened during my lifetime. In 1960 the trial of D.H. Lawrence's *Lady Chatterley's Lover,* hitherto banned for obscenity, ended in acquittal. Philip Larkin's *Annus Mirabilis* started:

Sexual intercourse began
In nineteen sixty-three
(which was rather late for me) –
Between the end of the Chatterley ban
And the Beatles' first LP.

William Golding's book *Rites of Passage* tells the story, written as a series of letters by a young man reporting to his godfather, of a voyage in an "ancient ship of the line" from England to Australia in the early nineteenth century. One of the passengers is the Reverend Robert James Colley. One day Mr Colley gets drunk and practises what the narrator calls *fellatio* (oral sex) on a member of the crew. When he sobers up, he is so horrified by what he has done that he retreats to his cabin, lies on his bunk, wills himself to die, and does so. The narrator reports:

In the not too ample volume of man's knowledge of Man, let this sentence be inserted. Man can die of shame.

I doubt whether this story would carry today the emotional charge that it carried even as recently as 1980, when the book was published, but our ambivalence about sex seems to continue largely unabated. On 27 April 2022, *The Times* gave over half a page of obituary to a lady known as Cynthia Plaster Caster. Her claim to fame lay in her making many plaster casts of penises, most in a state of erection, belonging to men with some of whom she subsequently slept. It was accompanied by a photograph of her, lightly dressed but with a finger to her lips and wearing a coy smile. Even though she was described as a "conceptual artist", it would have been inconceivable (and perhaps criminal) in my boyhood, and for many years thereafter, for something like this to be published in any newspaper, let alone *The Times* (which was then a staid broadsheet without pictures and with nothing but advertisements on its front page). So certainly this publication illustrates change. But the change does not push us much further towards an acceptance of sexuality as a normal and unremarkable feature of everyday existence. It shows instead that our attitude towards it is still characterised by a sort of brazenness, titillating and daring. If it isn't always dirty, it is at least naughty.

I don't claim to know why. What I do know is something so self-evident that it hardly needs to be said: that we apprehend sexuality in a way that differs radically from the way in which all the other animal species on the planet apprehend it. To them it is simply a natural, instinctive and straightforward feature of their lives. To us it is often a matter of almost constant and even obsessional preoccupation; it can inspire feelings of shame, grief, frustration, longing, disgust and antagonism; and it sometimes gives rise to acts that cause the actor's downfall (as in the case of the MP) and to acts that are criminal, including rape and even murder. And of course it can also give rise to feelings of joy, satisfaction and fulfilment. Or so it is said. At some time, perhaps, we shall come to terms with it.

For now, however, the strangeness of our attitude towards sex is undeniable. In our minds its importance is much exaggerated, but at the same time its practice is stigmatised. Among the many internet scams is one claiming to come from someone who has hacked into the recipient's system and who claims to be able to show footage both of the recipient masturbating to pornography and of the pornography concerned. The sender threatens to send these images to the recipient's contacts unless a bitcoin payment is made. This scam is apparently widespread, but of course both the claims and the threats are empty and the emails are sent purely at a venture. And yet … if there actually was some footage to show, and it really was shown, the victim would experience this as a terrible, embarrassing disaster; and this threat, if believed, can apparently lead to suicide. Put aside, for a moment, your learned attitudes to sexuality, and ask yourself why. The evolutionary purpose of sexuality is obvious, but what purpose can be served by our stigmatising of it?

Once I knew Francis Bennion, who died in 2015. He was a very considerable lawyer, an expert on statutory interpretation, and for many years one of the Parliamentary Counsel who draft Acts of Parliament. He was also a maverick, who brought a failed private prosecution against Peter Hain for advocating the disruption of sporting events in protest against apartheid. He was cantankerous and fell out permanently, and as a matter of principle, with anyone who annoyed him; and in due course he fell out with me. (Speaking of someone else with whom he had fallen out, he said, "It's a pity really, because I quite liked the chap".) But one of his books was called *The Sex Code: Morals for Moderns*. In it he argued (italics as in the book) that

> [W]e should *accept* our sexual nature, and correct the sex-negativism instilled by centuries of Judaeo-Christian teaching that sex is sinful … [and] … we should *fulfil* our sexual nature, in an ethical manner, and assist others to do the same."

As an aspiration, that is quite hard to fault. The book suggested also that it was not necessarily wrong for parents to have sexual intercourse with their children – a view which rested upon the view that such behaviour was not inevitably destructive.

Let one experience stand as an example of my own uneasy relationship with sexuality. When I was a law student, I stayed for a time in London at a small hotel in Bedford Place. I was lucky to have a car and I drove down each weekday morning to attend the premises of Messrs. Gibson and Weldon, law tutors, in Chancery Lane. It was so long ago that you could park for free anywhere in Lincoln's Inn Fields, something that would seem inconceivable today even if you could find a space to park in. Most days I went back to Bedford Place – you could park for free there, too – and walked across Southampton Row to have lunch in a café called The Green Parrot. Several times, as I crossed the street, I noticed a girl. She was tall, and so was I, so we could see one another over the heads of other people, and one day she came up to me and asked me the time. I fancied her very much, and I think she must have fancied me or she wouldn't have done this. And all I did was to show her my watch. She thanked me, and we parted. I knew that I couldn't chat to her because of my stammer and that even if she didn't reject me because of that she would certainly do so because of my sexual inexperience. This encounter must have happened over sixty-five years ago.

TEN

Free will – its non-existence

Of all the realities which humankind cannot bear, the non-existence of free will, and the corresponding existence of determinism, may be the most important and the most obvious. But I have found excuses to delay the work on this chapter and the next ones because I have tried already to cover their subject matter in two books, and I shrink from the task of doing it all over again – and in words that are both different and fewer. But I suspect that, like the shadows cast before by coming events, passages in my earlier chapters have already taken for granted the existence of determinism. I wonder if anyone has noticed. It would be interesting if they haven't: one of my contentions is going to be that, in living our ordinary lives, we assume the non-existence of free will, bringing the idea into play only when we need it in order to justify our retributive urges.

There is no reason to think that T.S. Eliot was himself a disbeliever in free will (not at all) but, having borrowed the title of this book from his *Four Quartets*, I'm going to quote some other lines from the same source:

Time present and time past
Are both perhaps present in time future,
And time future contained in time past.

Contrary to the strong, if incoherent, conviction of nearly all of humankind, I want to insist that free will, in its usual and popular sense, is quite clearly an illusion; and this, you could say, is precisely because time future (along with time present) is indeed contained in time past. I hope to clarify this thought, but there is a need first to clarify the meaning of "free will".

The popular, generally accepted, mainstream conception of free will could be summed up simply as *free choice*. The idea is that if any normal situation presents us with a choice as to how we might act, we really could and really might – might *really* – act in a way different from the way in which we do act. Our choice is free and unconstrained. The murderer might not have committed the murder; the politician might have told the truth and not the lie; the Post Office might have accepted that Horizon was full of bugs and tried to help the sub-postmasters instead of prosecuting them; and Hitler might shown benevolence towards the Jews and stayed out of the Sudetenland. This is the conception of free will that we have always at the back of our minds, the one on which the justice system is founded and by which the retributive punishment of criminals is said to be justified, the one on which we base our everyday dealings with other people, and the one on which the whole of our present moral dispensation is built. And it is this conception which, if rationality were to prevail, would come crashing down.

Some philosophers, the "compatibilists", adhere to a quite different conception of free will, one that involves no freedom of choice at all. They say that if we are free to do what we *want* to do – that's to say, what we have already formed an intention to do – then we have what they like to call free will. If we are sane, with no guns to our heads and no twisting of our arms, free from blackmail and other forms of coercion, then, in doing what we have formed an intention to do, we are exercising our free will. The murderer who intends to commit the murder and does so while sane and under no outside compulsion, can thus be said to do it of their own free will – and similarly with the politician and the Post Office authorities and Adolf Hitler. But this has nothing to do with free choice. To form a foundation for free choice – to justify retributive punishment for the murderer – you must at least show that the choice *itself* was free. It's no good showing that the choice, once made, was freely *implemented*. I'm going to argue that choices themselves are never free because they are imposed on the people who make them, not by coercion from outside, but by causation from within – by circumstance having made them the people they are. But these arguments would not trouble the compatibilist philosophers. They stick to their guns and write books in celebration of their conception of free-will-without-free-choice. Julian Baggini's *Freedom Regained: the Possibility of Free Will* is one such book, and I did my best to take it apart in one of mine.

Of course I'm all in favour of *having* the kind of freedom that compatibilists call free will. People living in democracies tend to take it for granted that they are free to do what they want (unless they want to do bad things, in which case their freedom may be constrained by outside authority), but those who live under repressive regimes may find themselves deprived of this freedom and may hanker for it and even die for it. No one doubts that compatibilist free will is a good thing: the question is whether it amounts to free choice, and of course it doesn't.

We should bear in mind what Humpty Dumpty said "in a scornful tone" in *Alice Through the Looking-Glass*: "When I use a word it means just what I choose it to mean – neither more nor less". William James called the compatibilist formulation of free will "a quagmire of evasion", and to Kant it was "a wretched subterfuge". But – and this is a big part of the problem – there is no universally agreed definition of "free will": if compatibilists want to define it in their way, and incompatibilists like me want to define it so as to embody free choice, what does it matter? Live and let live, you may say.

But it does matter, because there's a conjuring trick involved here. The question whether we have *free choice* is the all-important question, because so much is thought to hang upon it. The importance of this conception of free will – to us, to our institutions and to the whole moral dispensation within which we live – cannot be exaggerated. By contrast nothing of this kind hangs upon the compatibilists' conception of free will: no one in their right mind doubts that their kind of free will exists as a concept and (subject to exceptions) as a fact. But if you don't think too hard, it's not difficult to run the two conceptions together. If the compatibilists reassure us often enough that we have what they call "free will", it's all too easy to take this as confirming the existence of *real* free will. The two are as different as chalk and cheese, but there are some kinds of cheese that look, at first sight, quite a lot like chalk. And, to make matters worse, it's certainly true that we do sometimes, in everyday conversation, use the term "free will" in the compatibilist sense: if Dorothy makes a gift to charity, and we say that she did it "of her own free will", all we mean is that the gift was voluntary. And here's a quick definition of the difference between compatibilists and incompatibilists: to the former, free will requires only that an act be *voluntary* (as nearly all acts are); to the latter, free will requires that the act be *originated*, having its origins only in itself (as no acts are).

I've been speaking of "compatibilists" and "incompatibilists" without explaining these terms: what are their different views supposed to be compatible or incompatible *with*? And the answer is determinism. Confronted by this term, some people may feel their eyes begin to glaze over, but the idea is simplicity itself. Determinism is just causality: the familiar mechanism of cause and effect, the mechanism that children take for granted when they ask "Why?", and greet the answer with another "Why?" and the answer to that "Why?" with another. It's not rocket science. And of course it's a process that applies to everything: we couldn't live our everyday lives without it. In 1814, the French physicist, mathematician and philosopher, Pierre Simon Laplace said:

> We may regard the present state of the universe as the effect of its past and the cause of its future. An intellect which at a certain moment would know all the forces that set nature in motion, and all positions of all items of which nature is composed, if this intellect were also vast enough to submit these data to analysis, it would embrace in a single formula the movements of the greatest bodies of the universe and those of the tiniest atom; for such an intellect nothing would be uncertain and the future just like the past would be present before its eyes.

The hypothetical possessor of this intellect has come to be called Laplace's Demon. In 1936, Albert Einstein said, in a letter to a child who had asked him a question:

> Scientific research is based on the idea that everything that takes place is determined by the laws of nature, and therefore this holds for the action of people.

Each of us emerges from the womb with our own biological inheritance, and in each of us that inheritance develops and interacts with all the multitudinous influences that bear upon each of us as we grow up and grow older, ingesting and digesting values, beliefs, attitudes and information which may become unconscious but which combine to make us in every respect the people we are. These are the causes: we are their effects. By means of this subtle and endlessly complex process, any characteristics you care to name are built into us: religious belief or disbelief, criminality or rectitude, industry or idleness, empathy or callousness, understanding or crass ignorance. The events of time present and time future really are contained in time past. None of this, surely, should be controversial. You might even call it a glimpse of the bleeding obvious.

But we dislike the implications of it so much that we close our eyes to them. Not long before his death, Barry Cryer invented a good joke. It involves a married couple walking along a street and seeing, on the other side, a man waiting for a bus. The wife says to the husband, "That man looks exactly like the Archbishop of Canterbury". The husband says, "I see what you mean, but surely it can't be." The wife says, "Go across and ask him." So the husband crosses the street, speaks to the man, and comes back to the wife, who asks him what the man said. The husband replies, "He told me to fuck off." And the wife says, "Oh, what a pity: now we shall never know if it was him."

My narrative forces me to spell out the point of this joke, however obvious it is. The point, of course, is that if the man really were the Archbishop of Canterbury, he wouldn't have told the husband to fuck off. Why not? Because the causes of which the effect was the Archbishop of Canterbury did not build him in such a way that he would say this – unless, perhaps, illness had affected his brain, or he was for some reason in a vile temper, so that he acted completely out of character.

But if he had acted out of character for some such reason, he would not have stepped outside causality: on the contrary, we are still in the realm of cause and effect because it would have been some recent bit of causality that had determined his offensive behaviour: illness or ire. Determinism doesn't rule out changes of character, momentary or lasting, but the changes occur only if they are themselves determined. As Voltaire said, "Chance is a word devoid of sense; nothing can exist without a cause."

So the idea of determinism is simple enough: we behave as we do because our biology and lifetime experiences have made us the people we are, and in doing so have determined the way in which we behave. And really, of course, we *know* that this is so: when we are confronted by some appalling piece of human behaviour – a multiple killing, for example – we assume that the killer's reasons are to be found in his history. In this way we manage to hold in our minds two opposing ideas, because if the killer had free choice (as most of us would surely say he had, if we were asked) it would make no sense to search his history for his reasons. It's important to emphasise that compatibilists and incompatibilists do not disagree about determinism. What they disagree about is whether it is compatible with our having free will. Compatibilists say it is. Incompatibilists say it isn't. But they say these different things only because they have different conceptions of free will.

I must now nail my colours to the mast and say that the only kind of free will that matters, when it comes to our view of the world and the other people in it, is the normal, mainstream idea of free choice that I have tried to describe: incompatibilist free will. And what kills it is the fact that we do not construct ourselves, but are the products of biology and lifetime experiences – or, if you prefer, of heredity and environment; or, if you prefer, of nature and nurture (and there's always controversy about which of these two elements makes the greater contribution, but for our purposes it doesn't matter). These elements, and these alone, cause us to be the people we are and to behave as we do.

It follows that we *don't* have choices – or, to put it more accurately, we don't have *free* choices because, however many alternatives there may be for us to choose from, and however free we may *feel* when we make our decision, there's only one alternative that we are actually going to choose, and that's the one that our determined characters have determined us to choose. It's important to get this right. In the past some philosophers have proposed, as a test of free will, the question, "Could he or she have done otherwise?", but that's ambiguous. In most situations we could do otherwise if we had the physical ability *and we wanted to*. But it is the *wanting* that is both the determined and the determining factor. The philosopher Schopenhaur put this beautifully:

> You are free to do what you want, but you are not free to want what you want.

Here, perfectly expressed, is the difference between the compatibilists, who say that you have "free will" if you are free to do what you want, and the incompatibilists who say, no, not unless you are also free to want what you want. The hungry diner in my chapter on rationality, who preferred Chinese to Indian food, was not free to prefer Indian to Chinese.

And when Suella Braverman, then the Conservative Home Secretary, said that homeless people who lived in tents had made "a lifestyle choice", she may have been right in a sense – but not in the sense that their choice was a free choice, as she must have thought it was. But still (to be fair) the cruelty of her own remark was not a matter of free choice on her part either, because it sprang naturally from, and was determined by, her existing and un-self-created character. If free will were really to exist, there'd be no knowing what she might do next. Weep for the disadvantaged? Join the Labour Party?

Gary Neville, the former footballer, would probably not wish to claim affinity with Schopenhaur, nor Schopenhaur with him, but in September 2022 an interview appeared in *The Times Magazine* in the course of which the interviewer suggested that Neville might be working too hard, and he replied, "Yeah, the reality is I could change, but I don't want to change. My strength and my personality are such, I can only live the way I live." Exactly.

This question of choice may need to be clarified. Two books on my study floor assert the existence of choice when it comes to criminal behaviour. In one, a good book called *Unlawful Killings: Life, love and murder: Trials at the Old Bailey,* the retired Old Bailey judge, Wendy Joseph QC, says:

> For all the wrongdoers about whom I have told you, there's no doubt each took the decision to act and each must bear the responsibility for that. There is, after all, *always* a choice [her italics]. But if we think that is the end of the matter we are not just foolish, we are wickedly so. We are … closing our eyes to the obvious. Wrongdoers … are formed not just by their capacities but by their experiences … In some cases, if we are honest, we must accept that we have allowed them to become what they are.

And in her book, *What Lies Buried: A forensic psychologist's true stories of madness, the bad and the misunderstood,* Kerry Daynes records a conversation with Basil, a manager at a forensic step-down project, about a man called Stuart, an accountant who had killed his wife when she said she was leaving him for another man. The conversation goes like this:

> *Basil*: Stuart and I have spoken about his offence and he is deeply remorseful. He fully admits that the red mist descended.
> *Daynes*: Do you really believe in red mist?
> *Basil*: Don't you?
> *Daynes*: No, I don't. I believe that violence is a choice that people make when they are in a position of power over someone else. Granted, some people have more choices than others. I'm usually the first to point that out. But there is always a choice.
> And Basil (bless him) nods respectfully.

"Always a choice": what does this mean? Of course there are always two alternative courses of action: do the crime or don't do the crime. But is there ever (never mind always) a *free* choice between them? Both authors deal at length with the factors that go to produce criminals, but both seem to deny that these factors produce their crimes. If there is always a choice, how are these factors even relevant? Why mention them at all? Is the suggestion that, although they don't determine crime, they somehow make it "harder" to refrain from it? But choice is not dished out to different people in different quantities, like beer in a glass that may be half full, quarter full, or nearly empty. There is no such thing as partial free choice, let alone a kind of partial free choice that turns out mysteriously to produce just the same effects as full free choice. And over and above these thoughts hangs the basic question: why would, and how could, someone go against their own wishes and choose to do something they don't want to do? (And incidentally, I think Daynes is wrong to say that violence is always done by people in a position of power over others, and wrong to disbelieve in the red mist: it is surely true that many violent criminals act in the heat of the moment and without taking time out for decision-making.)

In rejecting free will, I am not alone but in good company. The number of philosophers who disbelieve in contra-causal free will is far and away the majority. Other disbelievers include the so-called celebrity determinists: Abraham Lincoln, Darwin, Freud, Mark Twain (an interesting one), Friedrich Nietzsche (who said, "The *causa sui* [to be the cause of oneself] is the best self-contradiction that has been conceived so far; it is a sort of rape or perversion of logic"), Bertrand Russell, Baruch Spinoza (who said, "The mind is determined to this or that choice by a cause which is also determined by another cause and so on *ad infinitum*"), and Voltaire and Schopenhauer, both of whom have already made an appearance in this chapter. And such great names as these are shyly joined by a number of ordinary people like me, including several that I know personally.

It's customary for determinists to call in aid the experiments of the neuroscientist Benjamin Libet, replicated by others. These demonstrate that the brain readies itself to do something just a little bit before we make a conscious decision to do it. So our decisions originate, not in consciousness, but in the unconscious. This is surely not surprising (although it surprised Libet), because unconscious motivation is all-important: you can seldom – perhaps never – express fully and truthfully the reasons for your own behaviour, as distinct from trying to rationalise it, because you just don't know what they are. Those who see Libet's results as confirming the non-existence of free will (and those who try to argue that they don't) are welcome to do so, but I see them as something of a sideshow, even a red herring. If you once accept that our behaviour is determined, it makes no difference how or where the determining takes place. Consciousness is not to be equated with free will.

The importance of unconscious motivation is nonetheless worth emphasising. It tends to be associated with Freud, but Freud did not "discover" it and it is now accepted fully by neuroscientists and psychiatrists. Freud likened the relationship between consciousness and the unconscious to that of a child sitting on an elephant. It is the elephant that decides which way to go and the child is a mere passenger: the child may suppose that he or she is guiding the elephant, but in truth is merely accepting and endorsing its decisions. We are not even in control of our own thoughts unless we set them upon some specific course. When Scarlett O'Hara in *Gone with the Wind* said, "I won't think about that today. I'll think about that tomorrow", the thing she didn't want to think about had already pushed its way unsought into her consciousness: otherwise she would have had no need to push it out.

A thought experiment provides a rather simpler confirmation of determinism. Imagine, if you can, two people who have had the same biological inheritance and the same life experiences and who are, as a result, atom for atom, brain and body, exactly the same. And both of them are faced with exactly the same choice between exactly the same alternatives. Do you think it possible that their choices will be different? Extend the thought experiment and imagine that it features twenty people or two hundred people. Do you think that any of them might choose differently?

Let's go back to the Barry Cryer joke. I've pointed out that the Archbishop might just possibly have told the husband to fuck off, so acting completely out of character, provided that there were some cause for his doing so, like being already ill or already angry. But just suppose that there was no such cause: absolutely none. Is it still conceivable that he would have told the husband to fuck off? Surely not. To suppose otherwise is to suppose that he stepped outside his normal self *for no reason at all*. But this, mark you, is exactly what belief in free will requires: that our behaviour is not determined by, but is detached from, our characters. If that were so, there would be no good people or bad people, but only unpredictable people making inexplicable choices.

Acting on the belief that free will must be a good thing to have (actually it isn't), some rather hopeless attempts have been made to preserve it. The philosopher Immanuel Kant, has appeared already in the chapter on perception. He pointed out that, because our perception of things in the outside world depended on the way in which our senses represented them to us, we could never perceive those things as they were *in themselves*. Things in themselves existed in what he called the *noumenon*, to which we have no access. So far, so good. But he went on to say that because – so he thought – our moral values must somehow be underpinned by free will, and because, as he fully recognised, free will did not exist in our everyday world, it must exist in the *noumenon*, where we could never find or understand it. This surely is a plainly flawed bit of reasoning. It is one thing to say that the *noumenon* contains the true nature of things that we misperceive through our senses, and quite another to say that it contains some unimaginable "mechanism" that has no counterpart in the everyday world and which, by its very nature, we can never understand. If I characterise this attempt to preserve free will as hopeless, I am borrowing the description given to it by the determinist philosopher, Ted Honderich.

Another hopeless attempt has to do with quantum mechanics – the strange behaviour of microscopic particles. Someone who had read my first book on free will started his online review: "This book is dreadful." He said so because he thought I should have paid more attention to this subject – and should, presumably, have drawn from it the conclusion that free will existed after all. It's true that the behaviour of quantum particles seems wholly unpredictable. The legendary physicist Richard Feynman said:

> Do not keep saying to yourself ... "but how can it be like that?" ... Nobody knows how it can be like that.

So Voltaire may have been wrong to say that *nothing* can exist without a cause, and perhaps Laplace's Demon would find himself at a bit of a loss in the microscopic world. Some of the behaviour of these particles does appear to be inconsistent with our conception of cause and effect (remember Schrodinger's dead and alive cat). But any idea that free will can be built on that foundation is plainly wrong. It seems clear that the behaviour of particles in the microscopic world has no effect on the macroscopic world in which we live and, even if it did, the effect would be only to generate behaviour which is random and unpredictable. There is a tendency to believe that, if only a hole can somehow be picked in determinism, free will is bound to rush in as air rushes in to fill a vacuum.

And of course there's always God. God is often said to have given us "the precious gift of free will". I don't believe in God, and so I haven't much to say about this. From where I'm standing, free will is an impossible concept that defies logic and reason. It would be a miracle if it were to exist. But God can do miracles, so presumably he could do this one. It's just a pity that he hasn't given us the means to make any sense of the idea. And it's a good thing we live in a secular society. Mind you, there may be doubt about the nature of the free will that God is said to have given us. In a short film in which the writer, singer and actor, Tayo Aluko, plays a priest, he says:

Free will is a gift given to us by God to act as we want.

But that's not real free will: it's compatibilist free will in a nutshell.

For completeness I need to mention that some people, convinced that free will itself cannot exist, are nonetheless keen to assert the existence of some sort of partial free will – to say that there must be "a little bit of free will in there somewhere". This idea is espoused by Bishop Richard Holloway. I like what little I know of Bishop Holloway: his agnosticism is as welcome as it is unexpected, and one of his books, *Leaving Alexandria,* is particularly lovely. But I really can't make sense of this idea of partial free will (any more than I could make sense, earlier in this chapter, of the idea of partial free choice, which comes to the same thing). All the objections to free will itself must surely apply in equal or greater measure to this idea of downsized free will. Even if it amounted only to a bit of wriggle room, there would still have to be a causal explanation for our wriggling in one direction rather than another. There is no stopping place between free will and determinism. And even if this idea of partial free will were coherent, its existence would be of no importance because we could never tell whether any particular human act was due to this unproven bit of free will (or, as I would say, this unproven bit of arbitrariness) or to the determinism in which, as its proponents would recognise, it is inextricably embedded.

I plan to suggest later on that we cling to the idea of free will largely because it seems to justify a lot of the savagery which is still latent within us. Apart from that, however, there is no reason at all to regret the non-existence of free will. It would be a strange and appalling thing to have, whereas determinism is a natural and comforting one. Determinism posits that we behave as we do because we are the people we are. There's nothing wrong with that. It does not invalidate our behaviour: it validates it. But free will, if it existed, would sever the connection between our behaviour and ourselves. We should be turned into strange and unpredictable creatures, acting in ways that would be incomprehensible to others and even to us. If we have the freedom that compatibilists call free will – the freedom to do what we want to do – what more do we want? The freedom to do what we don't want to do?

I can't claim to know how the idea of free will came to exist. I like to imagine a group of primitive human beings sitting round the camp fire and thinking about the misbehaviour of one of their fellows. Perhaps it was the one who, in my chapter about conscience, failed to join a head-hunting expedition. And when the rest of them feel the emotion which we would call anger, they make what we would call the unconscious assumption that this is because he really might have chosen to join the expedition. This assumption might have been reinforced by the illusion that they themselves had free choice – an illusion which we modern people still harbour today. But this scenario is, of course, pure fancy.

The first book by the neurosurgeon Henry Marsh was mentioned in my chapter about religion. While I was struggling with this chapter, I was reading his third book. *And Finally: Matters of Life and Death*. And now, as I reach the end of the chapter, I come by coincidence upon his thoughts about free will. He says:

Free will was a concept introduced by Catholic theologians to explain how evil arises in the world, despite a benign God. Although God is omnipotent, all bad things are our own fault.

And a little later:

Free will might be a legal necessity for an ordered society, but it is an illusion. Our decisions are determined by our past.

I'm inclined to question the first few words of this second quote, but we'll come to that. When I joined the staff of the Law Commission, one of the Commissioners was Norman Marsh, Henry Marsh's father. He was described as a great liberal lawyer by the Chairman, Leslie Scarman, later Lord Scarman, who was one himself. I remember clearly that Norman Marsh was once rather cross with me about something I'd been determined to do, or determined not to do, but I forget what it was.

When I was a small boy, I was habitually required to join my mother as she went shopping in the small town near our home. In trying to understand the world in which I found myself, I supposed that the people I saw had chosen to be in all respects exactly as they were. This idea became strained when I saw the crippled man behind the desk of the savings bank in Grenville Street (my mother said it was good of the bank to employ him), or the woman who owned the greengrocers in Mill Street and had a goitre that swelled her neck and affected her speech, or the young man in the shop at the other end of Mill Street who had a stammer like mine; but at the time I had no other explanation. In due course I learned of other explanations and I discarded this belief as

I grew up. Few adults harbour the belief that people choose their own bodies, although some people seem still to blame disabled people for being disabled. I myself discarded also the belief that people choose their own characters, but that belief is one that most adults seem still to harbour.

Free will is not something that might exist but just doesn't happen to do so. Unicorns don't exist, although they might: a unicorn wouldn't be a violation of nature. But free will couldn't exist because, as I've said, it would be a violation of reason and logic. If my decision to write this book is not determined by my being the person I am, then it is an arbitrary, inexplicable decision which can reflect no credit or discredit on me. Proponents of free will can't have it both ways.

Virgil rated the importance of cause and effect rather highly. He wrote:

> *Felix qui potuit rerum cognoscere causas*
> *Atque metus omnes, et inexorabile fatum*
> *Subjecit pedibus, strepitumque Acherontis avari*

This has been translated in various ways. I had to have extra tuition to get a Latin O level, which was necessary in those days to become a solicitor, but even I can see that the translation which follows is, to put it mildly, rather loose. But it's also rather lovely:

> Happy is he who can search out the causes of things,
> for thereby he masters all fear, and is throned above fate.

ELEVEN

Free will – the implications

So what? What does it matter if we don't have free will? Well, if we don't have free will – and we really don't – then nobody *deserves* anything: praise or blame, condemnation or adulation, punishment or reward, fame or infamy. And furthermore (as I plan to argue in the next chapter) there is no such thing as *moral* responsibility.

If all the writings of philosophers about free will were stacked up, they would reach the top, perhaps not of a skyscraper, but certainly of a sizeable block of flats. Isn't there something very strange – not to say downright wrong – about this? It isn't as if the existence of free will is an esoteric, academic matter of no practical importance: it is, or should be, of real significance to us as we live our lives. There is surely no other vital (and, I would argue, simple) aspect of our everyday existence that remains in doubt, and therefore ignored, because it is shuffled off to philosophers who continue to dispute it year after year after year.

How do we explain this situation? The explanation, I suggest, is that free will is not a philosophical problem at all. It is a psychological problem. It is psychological in the sense that the assertions made in the first paragraph of this chapter are simply unbearable to nearly all of humankind: to many (but by no means all) philosophers, and to most of the rest of us. John Horgan, former chief writer at *Scientific American*, has said:

Science has made it increasingly clear (to me at least) that free will is an illusion. But – even more so than God – it is a glorious, absolutely necessary illusion.

I'm quoting this comment, not with approval – I don't accept that free will is a necessary illusion, or that any illusion (including the illusion of God) can be described as glorious – but only to illustrate my point. Why does he say this? Presumably because the whole moral dispensation in which he has been reared and spent his life seems to him to depend on the existence of free will, and so he wants to uphold it, or at least the illusion of it. His statement is nonetheless a strange one for a science writer to make. He must surely have noticed that all those branches of science that concern themselves with human behaviour – psychology, psychiatry, criminology, anthropology, sociology, you name it – depend for their very existence upon determinism. If free will were to exist, none of them could exist.

A similarly-motivated wish to uphold free will is harboured by those philosophers who are programmed to dislike the kind of assertions made in my first paragraph. Some avoid the issue by taking refuge in a compatibilist version of free will. Others devise theories to counter the assertions, because that's what they *want* to do, and they hold to them with great tenacity no matter what other philosophers may say. Long ago I imagined that philosophers cast aside all predilections and concerned themselves only with pure rationality, but this just isn't so: I have read of no philosopher who, having set out to show that free will exists, has been forced by rationality to announce that it doesn't. The philosopher Tammler Sommers has been very clear about this:

Philosophers working on free will and responsibility proceed almost exclusively by appealing to intuitions

... and then developing theories to accommodate those intuitions.

This is, of course, a perfect description, not of reasoning, but of rationalising. A few of the rest of us do the same, but the vast majority accept the prevailing moral dispensation and never give the problem of free will a moment's conscious thought. The result, at the present stage of our civilisation, is that an incoherent, unexpressed idea of free will is still in the air we breathe, absorbed as we grow up, and almost never questioned – just as, in times past, the idea of religion was in the air that our ancestors breathed and went unquestioned by them. If it were not for our purely emotional resistance to determinism, there would be no doubt about its validity and no place for all the philosophical disputation.

But I think I am getting ahead of myself. I need to retrace my steps and come more soberly towards these conclusions.

I've been saying that free will is, or should be, of importance to us in our everyday lives. Strictly, of course, it isn't free will itself that's important, any more than a circular square would be important, because it doesn't exist: it's just an incoherent idea. What is important is our belief in the illusion of free will or, to be still more accurate, the supposed implications of that belief – what we take it to entail.

In the Pogues' song, *Fairytale of New York*:

The man sings, "I could have been someone", and the woman sings back, "Well, so could anyone."

And in 2012 the American Presidential candidate, Herman Cain, said:

If you don't have a job and you're not rich, blame yourself.

It's obvious that no kind of free will could allow us to transcend our physical or mental limitations. Whether we believe in what I'm calling free will – mainstream free will: free choice – or in compatibilist free will, our freedom to do things is limited in fact by our physical and mental capacity to do them. I couldn't run a mile (or even walk a hundred yards these days, certainly not without my stick), or be a mathematician or a theologian, and there's no brand of free will that could be said to change that. But believers in mainstream free will seem too often to be in denial about this obvious limitation: they seem implicitly to suppose that free will gives us not just free choice but the ability to achieve anything to which we choose to aspire. (So a man's reach does not exceed his grasp, but is always within it.) How else to explain these two quotes? Both illustrate the idea that free will is somehow untrammelled: that all of us can, and really might, cast off our natural endowments however limiting, our social status however low, our upbringings however abusive, our educations however inadequate, and all the other things that have built us to be the way we are – cast them off, and pull out of nowhere the motivation and ability to soar above them, leaving them far behind. And once you realise that this is simply not so, you are at least half way towards disbelieving in free will.

Whether or not we suppose that free will has these magical qualities, most of us are in no hurry to let go of it. When Christopher Hitchens used to say, "We must believe in free will – we have no choice", I supposed that he had coined this rather nice paradox himself, but apparently it originated with Isaac Bashevis Singer. However this may be, it is a further illustration of the wish, entertained even by those who understand the issues, to shrug off determinism and behave as if we really had free will. And it's true, I think, that Christopher Hitchens might have modified some of his more vituperative writing if he hadn't done this. But then again he might not, because accepting the non-existence of free will does not necessarily entail any change at all in one's outlook or behaviour. In the previous chapter, I quoted Baruch Spinoza as saying that "[t]he mind is determined to this or that choice by a cause which is also determined by another cause, and this again by another, and so on *ad infinitum*". Now I'll quote his next sentence:

This doctrine teaches us to hate no one, to despise no one, to mock no one, to be angry with no one, and to envy no one.

But of course we are taught many things, and some of them go in one ear and out the other, particularly if we don't want them to lodge in our consciousness because we don't like them. Two pre-conditions, it seems to me, must exist if the acceptance of determinism is to bring about any real change in any particular person. The first is that they accept it emotionally, and not just intellectually. And the second is that their conscience resonates with their acceptance and leads them some distance towards agreement with what Spinoza said. These two preconditions really boil down to the same thing, because conscience manifests itself emotionally. So the question is, how do you *feel* about determinism – about the fact that people's behaviour is determined by factors outside their control? Does this *matter* to you? Maybe it doesn't. Suppose, as a thought experiment, that I tried to convince Donald Trump of determinism and its implications. I'd have difficulty in getting him to listen, and I'd have more difficulty in getting him to understand, but even if I jumped those hurdles, it's very doubtful whether my unexpected success would result in his changing his outlook by a hair's breadth.

(You might like to personalise this thought experiment: there are many millions of people whom you could substitute for Donald Trump.)

I like to put forward another thought experiment. Aldous Huxley's *Brave New World* is set in the year 2540. Natural reproduction has ended and human embryos are produced in hatcheries and raised in conditioning centres from which they emerge as five different "castes", the lower ones with their intellects deliberately stunted. Now imagine an analogous but rather different scenario in which we are joined in our world by a new group of people. These others do not have natural births, upbringings and life experiences like the rest of us but, by means of a scientific process, they have been brought into existence, so constituted as we are constituted at the age of, say, 25. They seem the same as us, and their characters – their natures, their brains – are made to differ randomly among themselves just as ours do. Now suppose that one of them soon becomes a serial killer. This wouldn't be unexpected because a few people of similar ages in the existing population do become serial killers. Of course we should recoil from him, and of course we should have to apprehend him and deal with him in such a way as to ensure public protection and to reform him if possible. But would we think that he *deserves* punishment? (*Deserved* punishment is *retributory* punishment – a punishment inflicted to make someone suffer, or suffer more, simply and only because they have made others suffer.) Or would we rather say that he doesn't *deserve* this punishment because he is merely the product of the unnatural scientific process which has only recently brought him into existence with the mind of a habitual murderer? You'll see by now where this is leading, because surely there is no *relevant* difference between this killer and a killer from our existing population. Both have become killers, not by creating themselves as such, but as the result of a process. In the one case the outcome has been brought about by the luck deliberately built into the science, and in the other by the luck of biology and environment. If you think that this difference means that the one doesn't deserve retributive punishment, but the other does, I'd like to know why, because it doesn't seem that way to me.

But this is where conscience comes into the picture. Under our existing moral dispensation, and under the existing criminal law, people whose nature and nurture have programmed them with the desire to commit crime (and with no effective wish to refrain from it) are probably headed towards quite a lot of suffering – towards punishment that is *retributive*. Your own conscience may leave you happy with this result: you may see nothing wrong with it. Only if your conscience makes you feel that it cannot be right, cannot be justified, cannot be *fair*, will you feel inclined to react against it and realise that the punishment is not *deserved*. Donald Trump's conscience would probably not lead him to this conclusion.

The philosopher Neil Levy has pointed out that people whose lives are bleak and unsuccessful – poor, homeless, ignorant, dependent on benefits – suffer a double dose of unfairness. The first is the biological and environmental bad luck that has caused their plight. And the second is the denigration to which we subject them because of our belief that they could change their situation by a simple act of free will. This denegation is illustrated by an online comment made recently by a reader of *The Times*:

> I'm sorry, but I'll never support throwing money at people who don't want to work. Sitting at home all day, with free heating, sky TV, smoking pot and claiming 'anxiety', funded by people like me who work hard to pay our way.

This use of the phrase "throwing money at" is a good example of the way in which, as I suggested in my chapter on rationality, it is used as a rationality by-pass, and it sets the scene for the rest of the comment, which can best be described as imaginative. Of course it's true that nature and nurture have formed some people in such a way that they lead idle lives, and it's also true that things can sometimes be done to induce them to improve their situation, but both the idleness and the improvement are alike determined.

If you have struggled so far through this chapter, you may by now be frustrated and perhaps affronted. "That's all very well," you may say, if you are being polite, "but what follows from all this? Are we really supposed to live our lives according to Spinoza?" I think it is for each of us to give our own answer to this question. I emphasise the emphasis given by italics to two words in my first paragraph. The fact that nothing is *deserved* does not mean that we can, let alone should, treat all human behaviour with *laissez faire* indifference. Even if this attitude were justified, our natural feelings would not allow us to adopt it – if someone is dislikeable, we are going to dislike them, no matter that their dislikeability is determined – but of course the attitude isn't justified. We must, if only for pragmatic reasons, encourage good behaviour and discourage bad. And the fact that we are not *morally* responsible does not mean that we are not actually responsible in the sense of being the people who do what we do, and who need to be taken in hand if the things we do are bad and praised if they are good.

Have I, in those last few sentences, condemned to irrelevance all I have been trying to say in this chapter and the last one? I hope not, because that is certainly not my intention. For those who really *see* determinism, *see* the non-existence of free will, *see* and *feel* the implications, and bring their consciences to bear on them – for those people, the world shifts. It really does shift. They come to know what is wrong with our present moral dispensation, with the attitudes we bring to bear on other people and with the workings of our institutions. They can see that we have got it all wrong, all completely wrong. People better informed than me may know whether Spinoza managed to live according to the precepts he expressed (it seems unlikely), but humankind in general won't do so in the lifetimes of my great-grandchildren, if I have any, or in those of their great-grandchildren, if they have any. Still, I like to think that sometime, if humankind survives, we may get close to them. The philosopher Shaun Nichols is not encouraging:

> People just aren't going to change. The normal emotional and moral reactions we have are way deeper than all this theoretical speculation. Hume said basically that no amount of theoretical worrying is going to displace your natural moral sentiments.

But I'm rather less than half in agreement with this. It's certainly true that people "aren't going to change" any time soon. But over a long period people do change, and their "natural moral sentiments" do change. Look, for example, at their so-called natural moral sentiments about homosexuality, or couples living "in sin", or children born out of wedlock or, to go back further in time, about wife-beating (banned in London in Tudor times, but only because of the noise), about witchcraft, about burning at the stake, about bear baiting, about slavery or about the existence of the devil. Change is gradual, but it happens, and I think it happens because of a general increase in what can only be called understanding. If I didn't think that a general understanding of determinism might some day come to pass, and that it might reduce our cruelty to one another, I shouldn't be trying to write this stuff.

TWELVE

Moral responsibility

I had an impulse to start this chapter by saying: "The popular belief in moral responsibility is just another piece of human exceptionalism. We're only sophisticated apes, for goodness sake: why should we have moral responsibility?" But that might seem a frivolous thing to say.

Seriously, though, why have a chapter about moral responsibility? If determinism is true and free will is false – if we act as we do because we are the people we are, and we have not made ourselves the people we are – then we don't have moral responsibility. We are built to do what we do in a world built for us to do it in. Isn't it as simple as that? Yes, to my mind, it is; but most of humankind, including some philosophers, would find this conclusion unbearable, so more needs to be said. In 1983, the philosopher Peter van Inwagen wrote:

> To deny ... free-will ... is to deny the existence of moral responsibility, *which would be absurd*. Moreover, there seems no good reason to accept determinism.... Therefore we should reject determinism.... [I]t is conceivable that science will one day present us with compelling reasons for believing in determinism. Then, and only then, I think, *should we become compatibilists*.

The italics are mine. Surely this illustrates both the

incoherence of the idea of moral responsibility and the strength of the desire to preserve it at all costs. Van Inwagen says we cannot deny its existence. Why not? Just because he thinks it would be "absurd" to do so. And we must go through any contortions necessary to preserve it: by denying determinism itself if we can and, if we can't, by becoming compatibilists. We must do anything rather than accept that the real absurdity is the idea of moral responsibility itself. And it is wrong, by the way, to suppose that rejecting determinism would resurrect free will: it would give rise only to arbitrariness and inexplicability.

What is moral responsibility anyway, and why does it matter? Moral responsibility is important only because of what we take to be its implications – the consequences which seem to us to flow from it. For someone to be morally responsible for an act (or an omission, but I shall use the term "act" to cover both) is for them to be *deserving* of certain reactions to it – to make those reactions *justified* and *morally right*. If the act is good, then the reactions include praise, reward and celebration. If it is bad, they include hatred, condemnation and retributory punishment. Since we do in fact react in these ways to good and bad acts, the idea of moral responsibility seems to be necessary to preserve the moral dispensation under which we live, and that's why so many people can't let go of it.

In the last chapter I made the rather obvious point that, even in the absence of free will, we must, for practical reasons, encourage good behaviour and discourage bad – but that's a different matter. What I was saying there was that the preservation of our society depends upon our doing this, and so it must be done – done for pragmatic reasons, done as a melancholy necessity sometimes, you might say, although few people would think it melancholy. Certainly this amounts to *holding* people responsible, but that's not at all the same as their being *morally* responsible.

There are several varieties of responsibility. You may, for instance, be *actually responsible*, in the primary sense that it was you who did whatever it was that someone did. If you murder five people, you are actually responsible for their deaths, and this is true even if you are as mad as a hatter and believe that you are ridding the world of demons. Then, as I've just said, you may be *held responsible*. This happens if someone or some thing – a court, a tribunal, a jury – decides that it was you who did whatever it was (and they're probably right, but they could be wrong) and should face the consequences. Then you can *accept responsibility* – either because you are actually responsible or because you think you should behave as if you were. Ministerial responsibility – the responsibility accepted by a Government minister for a serious mistake in their department even if it was no fault of theirs – falls within this category, but we seldom see it nowadays. And then, of course, you can *feel responsible*. This is a description of an emotional state into which your conscience may plunge you if you are actually responsible, and sometimes even if you aren't, but one into which you probably won't be plunged if you happen to be insane. I mention these differing conceptions of responsibility only to point out that none of them amounts of itself to what we call moral responsibility.

So what is it that does give rise to moral responsibility? There can be only one answer and Van Inwagen gives it: free will. Our moral responsibility for doing any act can arise only if the act was not determined but freely chosen (so that we really might have done something else or done nothing at all) and yet – do mark this – it was not simply a random, undetermined act, but one that was unequivocally attributable to *us* in such a way as to reflect and shed light on *our* characters. But no such act could possibly exist: there is an inherent contradiction here. If we really are free to make any choice among several alternatives (the Archbishop of Canterbury choosing for no reason to tell the man to fuck off, or deciding to dance a jig or to urinate in the street) then the choice we make is by definition undetermined – not determined by our characters, not determined by our being the people we are. And if that is so then the act is necessarily an arbitrary, inexplicable act which can reflect no credit or discredit on *us*.

The philosopher Bruce Waller, who died in 2023, wrote a superb book called *The Stubborn System of Moral Responsibility*. In it he demolished the idea of moral responsibility and, although he was a determinist and a disbeliever in free will, he did it without overtly calling in aid the nonsensicality of free will or the validity of determinism. I was very grateful to know Bruce Waller a little, and I plucked up the courage to ask him why he didn't bring these things into the book. Because, he said, the default position of philosophers is to accept determinism but still to try to uphold moral responsibility. Oh, my goodness. There still exists a society to which the best professional conjurors belong and of which other conjurors aspire to become members. It's called the Magic Circle. Marvin Berglas, the conjuror son of the conjuror David Berglas, says he hopes to restore it to its former glory and to make it "more inclusive". I suppose it confers a status on conjurors rather like that conferred on barristers by becoming QCs – or KCs as they are now. And if these philosophers were to seek membership of the Magic Circle, they would surely be welcomed with acclamation because moral responsibility cannot be squared with determinism except by magic – and real magic, not sleight-of-hand magic.

A more recent book is *Determinism: Life Without Free Will*, by Robert Sapolsky, a neurobiologist and Professor at Stanford University. Armed with a wealth of scientific knowledge and a huge range of reference, he disposes of free will and has no qualms about rejecting moral responsibility along with it. He'd never get into the Magic Circle, no matter how inclusive it became.

What do you think about this yourself? Put aside thoughts of the pile of philosophical writings mentioned in the last chapter and make up your own mind. Recall, if you will, my thought experiment about the artificially-created serial killer: do you think he was morally responsible? A proponent of moral responsibility would have to say, yes, wouldn't they? How say you? Believe me, I have made an effort to understand how philosophers can uphold both determinism and moral responsibility, but I can't do it. Among the books I've read is *Just Deserts: Debating Free Will*, which consists of exchanges on this subject between two philosophers, the late Daniel Dennett, who believed in moral responsibility, and Gregg Caruso, who doesn't. It convinces me that Dennett had a powerful desire to believe what he believed, but not that his belief was coherent. Towards the end of the book, Caruso seemed to lose patience and sent him a message beginning:

> Your position, Dan, is like wrestling with an eel – every time I have a grip on it, or think I do, it slips out of my hands.

As Bruce Waller was, Gregg Caruso is a philosopher whom I know just a little and admire a lot. After the book just mentioned, he wrote another, *Rejecting Retributivism: Free Will, Punishment, and Criminal Justice*. It runs to 389 very closely printed pages which include 54 devoted to listing his references. It is a work of very remarkable scholarship. And I couldn't finish it. The problem wasn't that I disliked it: on the contrary I was pretty sure that there would be nothing in it with which (so far as my understanding went) I should venture to disagree. The problem was its very meticulousness. Every contrary argument, and every variation of it, was treated seriously, analysed carefully and rebutted at length, no matter how feeble the argument appeared to be.

At all events, it seems quite clear to me that, because we don't have free will, we don't have moral responsibility. But surely moral responsibility is in any case, like free will itself, an incoherent concept. It has no definition of its own, because it is always defined in terms of its supposed consequences. This is how I defined it earlier in this chapter and I have never seen it defined in any other way. And a concept defined only in terms of its consequences is locked together with those consequences in such a way that it must fall if they fall. And they do fall. Suppose that in fact free will were to exist and to be somehow coherent, so that the conditions for the existence of moral responsibility were fulfilled: would it even then be incontrovertibly *moral*, for example, to inflict retributory punishment on wrongdoers? Jesus would have said not. (Remember his insistence upon turning the other cheek?) There's a huge gap here. Even if free will really were a coherent concept, and we really did possess it, these supposed facts would not lead logically to the morality of retribution. It's an old and obvious philosophical truth that you can't get an "ought" from an "is": you cannot logically deduce a tenet of morality – a moral principle, a moral justification – from a mere factual state of affairs. And this gap consists in, and is filled by, our entrenched and largely unacknowledged *emotional* attitudes: we *want* to express our savagery towards wrongdoers, and we want to feel justified in doing so. This emotional but irrational desire is what fills the gap that logic leaves open and this is the basis for retributive punishment: there is nothing logical about it. And it is our emotional needs which blind us to the incoherence of the whole notion of moral responsibility.

But suppose that you really dislike (as you probably do) the idea that moral responsibility is a nonsensical concept. What can you do to rescue it? Van Inwagen gives you a clue: try to reject determinism. This isn't going to get you anywhere even if you succeed, but let's assume that you don't realise that yet, any more than Van Inwagen did. There are indeed some philosophers who do attempt this task, doing so by drawing a distinction between "responsibility" and "ultimate responsibility". Julian Baggini's book, *Freedom Regained: the Possibility of Free Will*, has already been mentioned, and he provides a very clear example. Baggini is a compatibilist philosopher who rejects mainstream – free choice – free will (and the italics are his):

> It rests on a naïve and simplistic assumption that we can rise above our biology and our history to make choices in a condition of unrestrained freedom ... [Who] we are appears to be a product of *both* nature and nurture, in whatever proportions they contribute, *and nothing else*.... And so, when you go on to make the choices in life that really matter [or, surely, the ones that don't?], you do so on the basis of beliefs, values and dispositions that you did not choose.

And, still better:

> Human actions flow inexorably from the characters of the actors as water flows inexorably from the source of a river. The only reason why we do not acknowledge this is that we do not feel any compulsion to act as we do. Our actions

appear optional to us because the forces that made them inevitable are not evident to us.

I want to give these extracts a prolonged round of applause: they are a clear and beautiful expression of determinism. But it seems to me that the logical conclusions are not drawn from them. On the contrary, Baggini still wants to cling to the old moral dispensation, so later on he seems to double back on himself and says this:

> Many arguments that purport to debunk free will are powerful only if you buy into the often unstated premise that real responsibility is ultimate responsibility. The [determinist philosopher] Saul Smilansky at least has the decency [*sic*] to make this assumption explicit. In what I take to be the ultimate example of the fixation on the ultimate, he writes: "If there is no libertarian free will, no one can be ultimately in control, ultimately responsible for [the] self and its determinations. *Everything* that takes place … ultimately derives from causes beyond the control of the participants."

And Baggini adds:

> I couldn't agree more, but read it again, removing all the 'ultimates', and the case weakens to the point of collapse.

He refers to his kind of non-ultimate responsibility (and of course it's *moral* responsibility that we're talking about here) as "partial responsibility" and, lo and behold, partial responsibility is then said to justify everything that ultimate responsibility would purport to justify: "ordinary punishment [which, he says, includes retributive punishment], praise or blame". So partial responsibility becomes the *same* as ultimate responsibility, because both are said to have the same consequences. Well, almost the same, because Baggini does identify one exception: that of "punishment without end ... eternal damnation". This, he says, would be justified by ultimate responsibility, but not by partial responsibility.

What on earth is Baggini thinking? Determinism is an intricate and continuous process of cause and effect, starting at fertilisation in the womb and going on (as Baggini himself has said) to form the personalities which we have at any given time in our lives, and so to determine our behaviour at that time. Since we do not ourselves create the factors which go into this process, we are not ourselves morally responsible for its outcome. So how does Baggini's "partial responsibility" come into this picture? Does he think that there is some stage at which determining factors weaken and something else begins to take over – but at what stage, and what is the something else, and why would this happen? His earlier comments suggest that he doesn't think that at all. So what, if anything, does he think? And what, when all is said and done, and all the chips are down, does it even *mean* for moral responsibility to be "partial"?

Perhaps Baggini, and other compatibilists who think like him, know the answers to these questions, but I'm not sure they do. I certainly don't. I think these philosophers are engaged in a rather clumsy bit of conjuring practised in the interests of preserving the present moral dispensation – a dispensation which, to my mind, is actually immoral – by means of a piece of word-play that seems plausible if you read it quickly but turns into nonsense when you think about it. His approach is a particularly good example of what Bruce Waller told me: that many philosophers accept determinism but still try to uphold moral responsibility.

The subject of free will and responsibility has dominated the last two chapters, and this one too, and it's going to spill over into the next one, so I wonder whether I can expect anyone to tolerate my saying any more about it here. But I would plead for tolerance, because there are a few things I need to say and haven't said yet.

In arguing against the concept of moral responsibility, I'm not arguing that the idea of *morality* – the idea that there are things we should do and things we shouldn't do – be simply abandoned. Of course not. I do think (and I hope to enlarge on this in the next chapters) that our justice system should be recast if it is to make sense, and the idea of *retributive* punishment abandoned, but sanctions against bad behaviour, and rewards for good, must obviously be maintained. What I'd like to see behind this necessary and pragmatic system of sanctions is a general recognition – a general understanding, a bit of overarching comprehension – of the fact that we are all of us, good bad or indifferent, the creatures of circumstance, and of the fact that, if we behave badly, our past circumstances are not excuses for our behaviour, but the causes of it. We sometimes speak of our "common humanity", and it is in this, perhaps more than in anything else, that it resides.

We often give *evil*, along with *wickedness*, a sort of supernatural overtone, as if evil or wicked people had chosen to do what was once thought of (and may sometimes be thought of still) as selling their souls to the devil. We suppose that being evil is a distinct state of being which they have deliberately embraced and to which they have consciously dedicated themselves – a state of existence which sets them apart from the rest of us. But why would they do this? To them, no doubt, evil behaviour brings some satisfaction, just as good behaviour brings satisfaction to other people, but evil behaviour usually makes the evil doers disliked and is often penalised. Would you choose to be evil if you had the option? My point, of course, is that the behaviour of "evil" people is no less determined than the behaviour of anyone else. Many people behave very badly indeed, inflicting death or great hurt on their fellow human beings and, like anyone else, I'm angered and horrified by what they do, but they do it because that's the way they're built. To label them as "evil" is just name-calling. I'd go further and say that it also serves to create a smokescreen between them and our understanding of their motivations and how they acquired them, an understanding that is necessary if "evil" is to be reduced.

What about the idea of *merit*? It is said that these days we live in a meritocracy. Actually, of course, we don't: merit does not guarantee us the acquisition of status or power or happiness, or of any of the good things in life: these are acquired, more often than not, by people to whom the idea of merit is foreign. It is true nonetheless that we cling tenaciously to the idea that merit should be rewarded, and from a pragmatic point of view this must be right. There is certainly no case for rewarding demerit, and it must be better to be governed by a meritocracy than by an aristocracy. But – and this is the point I want to make – it is absolutely wrong to suppose that meritocracy equates to *fairness*. The meritorious do not create their own merit. Merit is just as much determined by nature and nurture as nihilism, sadism, callousness or anything else. This fact is the concomitant of determinism, and the philosopher Galen Strawson expressed it better than anyone else when he said: "Luck swallows everything".

In May 2023, the *Sunday Times* carried a review of a book about the marriage of Nelson and Winnie Mandela. The reviewer referred to the ways in which "by the end of their marriage [Winnie] had become a monstrous figure" and went on:

The question is, to what extent can one make allowances given that she was so damaged and brutalised by the apartheid regime?

Perhaps this encapsulates what I have been trying to say in this chapter. Of course it would be of some interest to know just how the cruelties she had suffered after her husband's imprisonment had figured in the chains of causality that led to her becoming a monstrous figure. But why is this "*the* question"? There is implicit in this short quotation a belief in moral responsibility. The implication, surely, is that if these cruelties had caused her to become monstrous, she could be excused, but otherwise she couldn't. Why not? Because otherwise – the implication is – she must have become monstrous of her own free will. In truth, of course, the fact (if such it be) that her monstrousness was not caused by these cruelties would mean only that it was caused by other things. Determinism is true not only when the determining factors are obvious and inspire sympathy, but equally when they aren't and they don't. Yet the sentence that I have quoted from the review will have been read by thousands of people who have not questioned for a moment the assumptions behind it.

For many good reasons, we must surely bid farewell, as the sun sets and this chapter draws to a close, to the whole idea of moral responsibility. You may feel sad about this, and I'm sorry if you do, but that's the way it is.

THIRTEEN

Crime – irrationality and contradiction

This chapter and the next one are about the criminal justice system in the United Kingdom, which includes both the criminal law and the way in which convicted offenders are treated. To call this a "justice" system seems to me a misnomer, but we'll come to that. This first chapter is concerned mainly with a startling contradiction that lies at the heart of the system. There are basic and important aspects of it that depend wholly upon determinism and have nothing to do with free will, going so far as to assume its non-existence; but determinism is emphatically rejected in favour of free will when it comes to the conviction and sentencing of offenders. This inconsistency seems to go unnoticed: we find it hard to recognise, hard to bear.

Let me make it clear, first of all, that I'm concerned here with the enduring features of the system rather than with what might be called its present-day logistical problems. At the time of writing, these problems are very severe. The police are spattered with misconduct; they are failing even to investigate a range of crimes; the court buildings, those of them that are left after the closures, are in urgent need of repair; fewer and fewer solicitors can make their living on legal aid rates; and the number of accused people awaiting trial, often for years, is astonishing: in 2023 it stood at 410,000. After conviction, children are locked in their cells for 20 hours a day. Delays in the transfer to hospital of mentally ill prisoners have led them to block their own airways with bedding, remove their teeth and maim themselves to the point of exposing their intestines, often causing life-changing injuries. So it goes on.

The rule of law itself is not just endangered but severely damaged. This is a situation that few people seem to care about. One reason for failing to clear the huge backlog of cases is that the prisons, already full to capacity, could not accommodate the resulting increase in numbers. Prisoners are being freed early and at the time of writing (and it isn't April the First) the police have even been told to make fewer arrests. We have already the highest rate of imprisonment in all of Western Europe: some 88,000 people are now behind bars.

If more evidence of our savagery were needed, there it is. I have a file full of other cruel and counter-productive features of the present-day justice system, but other people have catalogued them and I shall put my file away in order to concentrate on the real subject of this chapter: the system's underlying structure and unspoken assumptions. These endure despite the current state of its logistics, but to my mind they are still more faulty and still more strongly to be condemned. T.S. Eliot would probably have disagreed. He doesn't seem to have been unhappy with the justice system: certainly its features can't have formed any part of the reality that he thought humankind couldn't bear. In 1923 we find him writing to the *Daily Mail* about Edith Thompson, who had been convicted of murder, along with her lover Frederick Bywaters, and sentenced to death. In his letter, Eliot congratulates the *Mail* on its insistence that she be hanged, as indeed she was, and says that its attitude is in striking contrast with the flaccid sentimentality of other papers I have seen, which have been so impudent as to affirm that they represent the great majority of the British people.

Eliot seems to have been having an off day both as a writer (it's hard to see how sentimentality can be "flaccid": it would be pretentious to put a psychoanalytic interpretation on this bit of phraseology) and as a fair-minded man, let alone a compassionate one, because the conviction of Edith Thompson was widely thought even at the time to be wrong, and it has been thought so ever since. *The Times* recorded in January 2023, one hundred years after her death, that a group of people had gathered at the City of London cemetery in memory of Edith Thompson, described as "a woman thought to have suffered one of Britain's gravest miscarriages of justice". They sang *Abide With Me* and heard a eulogy, and they had hopes that she might sometime soon be pardoned. Her case has now been referred to the Criminal Cases Review Commission.

If the public were concerned at the time about Edith Thompson, this was only because the evidence in her particular case was vanishingly weak – they weren't worried about Frederick Bywaters – and in general they were no doubt at one with Eliot in his approval of hanging. Even today, many people in the United Kingdom (to say nothing of those in America and other countries in which capital punishment still exists) would share their approval. Less than a month after the gathering at the City of London cemetery, the newly appointed and subsequently disgraced Deputy Chairman of the Conservative Party was quoted as backing the death penalty "for its money-saving potential and '100 per cent success rate' in preventing reoffending". And in August 2023, a poll taken after the conviction of Lucy Letby (for killing seven babies and trying to kill another six) found that 49 per cent. of the public wanted the death penalty to be restored for any murder. More wanted it restored in the case of particular categories of victim: 52 per cent. for a "Royal" victim, 54 per cent. for a police victim, 59 per cent. for multiple victims, and 63 per cent. for a child victim.

Raymond Chandler, the American author of detective stories, was described in the *Literary Review* as "one of the finest prose writers of the twentieth century". In a story called *Goldfish* (because – spoiler alert – stolen pearls were hidden in the fish), his creation and narrator Philip Marlowe has injured a very bad guy called Madder:

> I went back to the fish room. Madder was groaning now, thick panting groans. What did I care about a torturer like Madder?

And later:

> I looked at Madder, at his little pain- and fear-tortured eyes, the sweat on his face. I didn't care anything about Madder. He was a killer, a torturer.

Probably no one questioned Marlowe's attitude towards Madder: it would have seemed right and proper. But pause for a moment. Did Madder create himself as a killer and torturer? Did a law-abiding Madder wake up one morning and decide to become a torturer and a killer? Bearing in mind that having these propensities was likely in the end to be a very bad deal for him, as indeed it was, he would have been unwise suddenly to adopt them. No; Madder was the creation of circumstance, and no one would wish upon a star to be like him. I have heard (so, probably, have you) criminals described as "born evil" – described like that in a tone of outraged condemnation, as if they had been bad fairies cursing themselves at their own births. If it were possible for someone to be a criminal simply of his own inborn nature (and I mention later some research which seems to show that it is), he would surely be born ... well, evil if you like, but also very unlucky indeed. So, too, of course would his later victims be, and you can be as angry about that as you like, but their misfortune would not cancel his. And having just mentioned Lucy Letby, I might add that the same questions could be asked, and the same things said, about her – or about any other malefactor you might care to name.

In trying to account for the retributive attitude of T.S. Eliot and Raymond Chandler (or Philip Marlowe) and those who thought like them, and the very many who still do, several chapters of this book are relevant. Their attitudes have something to do with irrationality, conscience and misperception; they have a lot to do with savagery; and they have to do, above all, with the incoherent ideas of free will and moral responsibility. I say that these ideas are incoherent, but they are nonetheless powerful. Just as religious belief plays a big, if often unacknowledged, part in human behaviour even though religion itself is (as I would argue) a nonsense, so free will and moral responsibility do the same – and nowhere more than in our attitude to crime – even though the concepts themselves have no place in reality.

There's a man crouching just after midnight beside a large house. He's been watching it for a while, and it seems for the moment to be unoccupied, but it certainly isn't empty: on the contrary, it looks as if it contains a lot of valuable loot. The man is a habitual burglar. I shall call him X, but that is not his real name. X makes his living by breaking into houses and stealing what's inside. He feels no guilt at all about doing this and will feel no remorse when he's done it, and at the moment he's short of money. So X has a wholehearted desire to break into this house and no qualms about doing so. Suppose he does break in, and suppose that the house is occupied after all and that a child wakes up and is traumatised by seeing him. What are we going to feel about this? Most of us, surely, are going to feel that he *deserves* to be punished rather severely. Why? Because he didn't need to break in. No one forced him to break in. He broke in – here it comes – of his own free will.

And we should be in distinguished company. Lord Bingham of Cornhill, successively Master of the Rolls, Lord Chief Justice, Senior Law Lord and Senior Justice of the Supreme Court, author of *The Rule of Law* which won the Orwell prize for literature, has been described as the greatest lawyer of his generation. In a 2007 case called *R.* v. *Kennedy* he said:

> The criminal law generally assumes the existence of free will. The law recognises certain exceptions, in the case of the young, those who for any reason are not fully responsible for their actions, and the vulnerable, and it acknowledges situations of duress and necessity, as also of deception and mistake. But, generally speaking, informed adults of sound mind are treated as autonomous beings able to make their own decisions how they will act ….

I have to register a quibble here because autonomy (which I'm all in favour of) is not at all the same thing as free will, but that's a side issue. Clearly Lord Bingham is speaking here of what I've called mainstream free will, and of course he states the law correctly, and most of us would think that the law is itself correct. But I don't think it is, and I invent the rather plausible story about X, the burglar, in order to make some obvious points. On the facts I've given, there isn't really any chance at all that X won't break in. If he were to find himself coming out of concealment and going home instead, no one would be more astonished than he. All the determining factors point to his breaking in and there are none to point against it. So we can predict, can't we, that he's going to do it? Well, we can unless we really do believe in free will. Free will means *free choice*, and free choice is *undetermined* choice – a choice free of determinism, free of the ineluctability of any chain of causality.

The law, endorsed by Lord Bingham, assumes that X might really exercise his free will and walk away, and most of us assume the same: *that's why we blame him when he doesn't*. But if in these circumstances X might really do this, then prediction would be impossible. He would be behaving in a way in which he had no reason, no motivation and no wish to behave, and if X might behave in such a way then so might anyone and no one's behaviour could be predicted. Prediction depends upon causality, and free will negates causality. But we don't want to accept this because we want to believe *both* in predictability *and* in free will. And so, being human, we have created a justice system that relies upon both, a system in which free will and determinism, mutually exclusive though they are, contradictory though they are, nonetheless go hand in hand.

My contention – and this will come as no surprise – is that all crime is determined. There is no place in the justice system (or anywhere else) for the idea of free will. If the behaviour of criminals were not determined, there could be no justification for labelling any criminal as dangerous or for supposing that, without the law's intervention (perhaps even with it), any criminal, however habitual, would continue to re-offend. For why should the habitual criminal not freely decide to kick his habit and live a law-abiding life, and the dangerous criminal to stop being dangerous and become admirable instead? Most of us would say, if pressed, that they really could and really might turn their lives around in just this way, and we hold them morally responsible for their wilful refusal to do so. We expect miracles from free will, as we do from God, despite the non-existence of both. And if these *volte-faces* were a real possibility then, as I suggested earlier, the sciences of criminology and penology could never have existed and there could be no explanations of criminality. Just as (so it was said) love means never having to apologise, so belief in free will means never being able to explain. If you believe in determinism, human actions are (in principle, if not always in practice) explicable: a complex chain of cause and effect must lead to them, and lead back from them. But if you believe in free will – in free choice – then there is no such chain. For a believer in free will, it is futile to ask why anyone does anything. Free will closes the book of explanations. Nothing but causality will open it.

So, let's have a quick recapitulation. The idea of free will? It's incoherent because it defies logic and reason; it is nonetheless believed to generate deservedness and to justify retribution; and an act done in the supposed exercise of free will would be undetermined and therefore of its nature unpredictable. The idea of determinism? It's entirely coherent because it relies on the familiar mechanism of cause and effect; it does not generate deservedness or justify retribution; and a determined act is (in principle and often in practice) predictable.

Let us now get down to brass tacks and take a hard look, first of all, at some of the ways in which the criminal justice system relies on determinism and ignores free will.

When offenders sentenced to life imprisonment have served the term that they must serve before being considered for release, the decision about their release, taken by the

Parole Board, depends upon the making of a prediction: are they now safe to be at large? And if they are released, they are then supervised by the Probation Service whose continuing job it is to predict whether they are safe to remain at large. Sometimes the predictions are wrong. This happens because the evidence that leads to the prediction is faulty or inadequate or just doesn't justify the prediction made. In the case of the Probation Service, this in turn may be because – here's another logistical problem – the service is starved of resources. Whatever the reason, my point is that, in this very important area, the justice system is in fact constructed on the basis of *determinism, not free will.*

This is the place to mention something both interesting and shocking: the IPP (Imprisonment for Public Protection) sentences. Without going into too much detail, these were imposed on a convicted offender when the court foresaw

a significant risk to members of the public of serious harm occasioned by the commission by him of further specified offences.

In these circumstances, the courts were obliged to impose a sentence of imprisonment for *life*, and at the same time to fix a minimum sentence (the "tariff") which offenders must serve by reason their current offences. After that it was up to the Parole Board to decide when, if ever, they were safe to be released – and if they were released they could be recalled to prison for minor misbehaviour such as failing to find suitable accommodation. In practice IPP prisoners had little or no opportunity to show that they were safe to be released or to undergo any courses that might make them so. These sentences, the brainchild of David Blunkett (who became Lord Blunkett and later admitted that he had been wrong) were created in 2003 and abolished in 2012, but the abolition was *not retrospective*. As a result, some 2,800 IPP prisoners remain in goal, some mutilating themselves in their despair. The number would be larger if 287 hadn't died, 90 of them by their own hand. Aaron Graham had a tariff of just over two and a quarter years and he's still in prison 20 years later. Martin Myers had a tariff of just under than 20 months: he was let out after 17 years but sent back to prison for taking Valium to relieve his anxiety.

The IPP sentences provide another good example of our savagery, but how are they relevant in the present context? IPP sentences involve prediction by the Parole Board and the Probation Service, but we've looked at that already. What is interesting about these sentences is that they provide a striking example of prediction by the *courts*. Judges were supposed to decide whether offenders posed the "significant risk" described above. Everything turned on this because IPP offenders were to be punished, not for anything they'd done, but for what they might in future do. Presumably the judges who were charged with this task accepted the general view that the offenders had committed their current offences through an exercise of free will, but in order to make the necessary predictions they were bound to set aside all thoughts of free will and assume that future offending was determined by past offending.

What might these judges say, along with members of the Parole Board and the Probation Service, if taxed with the idea that their work was founded on a denial of free will? Probably they would stoutly deny their denial. "Oh," they might say, "we aren't denying offenders' free will: we're just predicting the way in which they will exercise their free will". OK, but how is that to be done? "Oh, well, we look at their past offending. We hear (if we can) from prison officers and others who have known them well. We decide what sort of people they are. We look at their circumstances. We assess their propensities. And so forth." But hang on: the things you are considering are all *determining* factors. To suppose that you can predict how people will exercise their free will is to assume that they have no free will to exercise.

In 1985, a civil court decided the case of *Meah* v. *McCreamer*. Mr Meah had suffered a head injury through the bad driving of Mr McCreamer. This injury had changed his whole personality, and he sued for compensation. Nothing strange about that; but one of his heads of claim was that whereas, before the injury, he had had only mildly criminal propensities, he had now become a violent criminal and had assaulted two women, raped another, wounded all three, and received a sentence of life imprisonment. For this life sentence, he claimed compensatory damages, and he got them. No one suggested that he should have used his free will in order to refrain from the violence: the judge found that his violent criminality was simply determined by his head injury. Two points are worth noticing. The first is that, despite his crimes being determined in this way, he was still held morally responsible for them and punished very severely. There might be something wrong with that. The second is more interesting. Even before his injury, Mr Meah had been a petty criminal, and the judge in his civil case reduced his damages on the ground that his life of petty crime would have continued even if he had had no head injury, and that he would therefore have spent part of his life in prison anyway. This surely was a deterministic prediction to top all such predictions: a prediction not only that Mr Meah would have wanted to go on being a petty criminal, but also that *nothing the criminal courts could have done would have stopped him*. The judge assumed not only the validity of determinism, but also the total failure of all available criminal sanctions to break into, and become part of, the chain of causality in order to deter Mr Meah, or to reform him. If the civil judge ever ran into his colleagues from the criminal courts, one wonders what they said to him. Perhaps, in their heart of hearts, and with the limited options available to them, they knew he was right.

Another example of reliance on determinism is provided by the Domestic Violence Disclosure Scheme ("Clare's Law") which allows people to find out from the police if a current or former partner of theirs has a history of violence or abuse. In October 2023 a police force was found to have failed to respond to many people applying for this information. There would of course be no point in obtaining it if free will washed away all likelihood of the partner's misbehaviour in the past being repeated in the future.

Just to put the tin lid on this subject, I should record that software now exists to predict the future behaviour of criminal offenders. There is, for example, the "harm assessment risk tool" which helps police to decide whether people in custody are at serious risk of reoffending. The predictions made by this piece of software were found to be better than the predictions made by the police themselves. Both did the job rather well: 89.8% and 81.2% respectively. I don't think either of them factored free will into their calculations.

In these and other ways, the justice system implicitly assumes that determinism rules. But in other respects, and with deep inconsistency, it throws determinism out of the window and pretends that it is free will alone that rules. Let's see.

Any defending advocate (perhaps speaking only in mitigation) who was foolish enough to suggest that their client's actual crime was *determined* – that the client was built to commit the crime in a world built for them to commit it in: that it was *predictable* that they would do it – would be laughed out of court or, more probably, criticised. But there was an advocate who did exactly this: the American attorney Clarence Darrow. (He was played by Spencer Tracy in the film *Inherit the Wind,* about the 1925 Scopes Monkey Trial in Tennessee.) As a determinist, he would defend his clients with long speeches in which he sought to destroy free will and moral responsibility. In 1888 he summed up his views in this way:

> The worst of all cruel creeds and of all bloody wrongs inflicted by the past can be found in the barbarous belief that man is a free moral agent.

I feel the need to express my own belief that he was absolutely right, and I should rather like the reader to take a short break in order to digest this. As one might expect, however, Darrow's advocacy was not uniformly successful.

Samuel Butler's novel *Erewhon* was first published in 1872. Its protagonist crosses a mountain range and comes upon an undiscovered country. When he explores the attitudes and customs of its inhabitants, he finds them very strange. For example, illness is regarded as a crime to be punished, whereas what we would call crime is treated as an illness deserving of sympathy. This attitude towards crime serves to "prevent [other people] from even thinking of treating criminals with that contemptuous tone which would seem to say, 'I, if I were you, should be a better man than you are'". This captures exactly the attitude which at present we really do display towards criminals. Let this thought – *if I were you, I should be a better man than you are* – marinate for a few moments. If we analyse it, we can see that it's crazy; but we don't analyse it; we don't even express it in words; yet we harbour it nonetheless: in fact, we harbour it all the more. If I were you, of *course* I shouldn't be better than you: I should be just the same as you and I should behave just as you do – and that's determinism. But we just don't see it like that because we believe the unbelievable: we believe in free will.

Samuel Butler's novel is remarkable, by the way, for having predicted the anxiety now widely felt about the future evolution of artificial intelligence. The Erewhonians hated and feared "machines", thinking that they would evolve to the point of challenging human supremacy; and all their more complicated machines had been destroyed before the action takes place.

It seems that the *penal* branch of the justice system – the acts that are labelled as crimes, their nature, their ingredients and what happens to people who commit them – must have been designed by believers in free will, even if they had a lingering foot in the determinist camp. It is here that determinism starts to be jettisoned and free will starts to take over. Let's begin with the official statement of "the purposes of sentencing" for adult offenders, which is now to be found in section 57(2) of the Sentencing Act 2020. I'll set it out and add some comments:

The court must have regard to the following purposes of sentencing -

(a) the punishment of offenders,

Years ago, before they were enshrined in statute, textbooks listed the purposes of sentencing under the general heading of "Punishment". In order to distinguish this one from the rest, they called it "Retribution", and this is exactly what it still is. Punishment for deterrent purposes is listed separately.

(b) the reduction of crime (including its reduction by deterrence),

Deterrence is the important word here. It has two aspects. First, the deterrence of the offender from further crime; and second, the general deterrence of other people from committing crimes. Although this head only "includes" deterrence, it is hard to see what else it might cover. Of course there are many other things – vital things – that could be done to reduce crime, but they can't be done, under the present regime, by sentencing individual offenders.

(c) the reform and rehabilitation of offenders,

This, to my mind, is the most important aim. In so far as it succeeds, its success benefits both the offender and the public.

(d) the protection of the public,

This has to do with the confinement of offenders who are dangerous.

(e) and the making of reparation by offenders to persons affected by their offences.

The idea behind this aim is fair enough, although full reparation is seldom a possibility.

Here we still find the dichotomy that I've been talking about. There is, for example, a clear contradiction between head (a) and head (d). The idea that retribution is a desirable aim of sentencing is founded on the concept of deservedness, which stems from belief in free will. By contrast, the idea that offenders are "dangerous", so that the public needs continuing protection from them, is founded (as I've already said) on the concept of predictability, which stems from determinism. It's arguable, too that heads (b) and (c) rely more on determinism than on any idea of free will.

But there is an important reason why, like the name of Ben Adhem in Leigh Hunt's poem *Abou Ben Adhem*, the first of these leads all the rest: retribution dominates all the rest, both in the public mind and in the justice system. This head – retribution – and much of the criminal law itself are so constructed as to depend wholly upon the validity of free will. And it is this construction – its pointlessness, its inherent unsustainability, and (if you will forgive me) its sheer inhumanity – that demands the making of radical changes to the criminal justice system. As matters stand, criminals' supposed deservedness of retributive punishment is overwhelmingly important to people in general. It is so important that we can't let go of the free will that underpins it, even though (as I hope to show) its preservation depends on the belief that it can be chopped into little bits of decreasing size, rather like the smaller and smaller versions of itself that we find inside a Russian doll.

Anyone who has read Leigh Hunt's poem about Abou Ben Adhem may recall that he "awoke one night from a deep dream of peace and saw … an angel writing in a book of gold". Some sixty years ago, Staff Sergeant Willis Boshears awoke from what he thought was a deep dream and saw to his surprise that he appeared to have strangled a woman called Jean. He panicked and tried to dispose of the body, but when he came to trial he convinced the court that he really was asleep when he killed Jean, and he walked away a free man. His defence, advanced on a few other occasions by people accused of murder, is known as "sane automatism". Bear this case in mind, if you will, because I plan to bring it up later on.

In order to demonstrate the importance of deservedness grounded in free will, let us suppose that you are charged with a murder. If you're found guilty, you will receive a sentence of life imprisonment. What this means in practice is that the judge will sentence you in accordance with guidelines now set out in Schedule 21 to the Sentencing Act 2020. If the "seriousness" of the offence is "exceptionally high", according to scenarios set out in the guidelines, this may be a "whole life" sentence, and you will never be released at all save in the most exceptional circumstances. But in cases of less "seriousness", the sentence will require you to serve a minimum number of years, variable according to scenarios also set out in the guidelines (and variable still further according to seven aggravating factors and seven mitigating ones) and after that you will be released if and when the Parole Board thinks it safe; and if you are released, the Probation Service will supervise you and see that you go back to gaol if you misbehave.

But what is "seriousness"? According to section 63, it's a combination of two things: the offender's *culpability* and the *harmfulness* of the offence. In practice, culpability plays the bigger part in the guidelines (and all the more so because harmfulness itself includes not only harm done but harm *intended*, so that what's a mere thought in your head goes to increase your culpability) and culpability is just another word for what I've been calling deservedness. I don't want to make this too tedious (it may be rather tedious already and I'm sorry), so let's take just one example.

Suppose your family has suffered harm at the hands of a 17-year-old tearaway called Y (not his real name either). He's a very nasty piece of work – the work not his own, of course, but that of nature and nurture. You are driving along a deserted street one dark evening and you see Y in front of you. On an impulse, you deliberately run him down, killing him, and drive away. The starting point for your sentence will be 15 years. It may be increased because of Y's age, but reduced because there was no premeditation. Exactly the same sentence will follow if you stop the car and strangle Y, hit him with a sledgehammer or stab him with a kitchen knife left over from a picnic. But if the knife you stab him with is one you carry as a weapon for self-defence, the starting point nearly doubles to 25 years. And if you shoot him (even with a gun that's in your car only because you've been on a grouse shoot), the starting point goes up to 30 years. It does so, too, if his skin colour is different from yours and the killing is racially "aggravated".

Up to now, however, we've assumed that your murder of Y was committed on the spur of the moment. Relatively lucky for you if it was, because if it was planned or premeditated then, no matter what the method, you'll receive a whole life sentence and you won't get out of gaol alive. And the same result will follow if it was sexually or sadistically motivated. But if Y had been 18 instead of 17, the starting point would go back to 30 years even if his murder was sexually or sadistically motivated, and premeditation would be only an "aggravating factor". (As I write, the government seems to be proposing that sexual or sadistic motivation should result in a whole life sentence whatever the age of the victim – a change that may seem logical but has nothing else to commend it.)

In his book, *An Uncommon Lawyer*, Lord Woolf, another judge who became Master of the Rolls, Lord Chief Justice and a Law Lord, tells us that these guidelines were enacted at the behest of David Blunkett when he was Home Secretary. The Human Rights Court had said it was wrong for a Home Secretary to determine the length of a life sentence because he was not sufficiently independent. Lord Woolf says:

David Blunkett ... was not prepared to take this decision lying down, so he inserted into his Criminal Justice Bill ... a schedule [that now appears in the Act of 2020] ... This was an approach that did not conflict with the Convention on Human Rights ... [It] was, however, a huge mistake and condemned this country to continuous overcrowding in our prisons, which made rehabilitation difficult, if not impossible. The periods which were set down ... were substantially longer than would have been recommended by an independent judge.

Lord Woolf is on record also as saying more generally:

Sentences are double what they were when I become a High Court judge [in 1979]. It is really sad. Sentencing is now hugely penal. There is no doubt about it. It is more punitive than in the past.

In January 2024, Lord Phillips of Worth Matravers, a former President of the Supreme Court, said that "we lock up people for far too long"; that even the meagre facilities provided in prisons were wasted by "locking up people when they're not a danger, when they've been in prison for some years by way of punishment"; and that "a system that locks people up like animals in cages for 23 hours out of 24 is basically inhumane". These comments are not just impressions, by the way: in 2023, the Sentencing Council found that sentences imposed in the crown court in 2022 were 38 per cent. more severe than those imposed even as recently as 2002.

And in November 2023 – do get this – a German court refused to extradite an accused drug trafficker to the United Kingdom because of its concern about the condition of our prisons. At the Conservative party conference in 2023, the Justice Secretary said that the government would be entering exploratory discussions with potential partner countries in Europe to rent prison space abroad. Agreements would mean, he said, that UK prisoners could be moved to foreign prisons provided that "the facilities, regime and rehabilitation provided meets British standards". Many countries would need to drop their standards a long way in order to meet this criterion.

But perhaps I digress. Does my example of the different sentencing scenarios, described above, make any sense to you? They are hard to defend on any basis, but they seem to have more to do with culpability than with harmfulness. For example, the fact that the death was premeditated makes it no more harmful, so it must be thought to increase your culpability. So also must the fact that you get sadistic pleasure from it. In fact, of course, it is not your fault that you are a planner or a sadist. Nothing but belief in free will can have led Blunkett to think it was. Ah, you may say, but some of these variations have to do with deterrence: perhaps, for example, Blunkett wanted to hit gun crime murders particularly hard, and knife crime murders not quite so hard, because he wanted to deter people from carrying knives and guns. But there are two objections to this idea. One is that the guidelines deal only in culpability and harmfulness, not deterrence. The other is that would-be killers seldom study and take into account the details of Schedule 21 to the Sentencing Act (it took me a long time to understand them, and I'm supposed to be a lawyer), they usually act impulsively without thinking at all and, even if they do think, they don't expect to be caught – and why should they when, as is now the case, ninety per cent. of crimes go unsolved?

But we may be getting ahead of ourselves because, even if you are shown to have killed someone, you won't necessarily be convicted of murder. It is here that the idea of free will dominates most obviously. Remember Staff Sergeant Boshears: if you did a killing in your sleep, you go free. The killing of Jean was certainly harmful even if it wasn't culpable, but a successful defence of sane automatism secures acquittal because it negates what lawyers call *mens rea*: Boshears had no "guilty mind" and therefore no conscious intention to do Jean any harm.

Nor will you be convicted of murder, whatever your mental state may have been at the time of the killing, if you are grossly psychotic and "unfit to plead" when you come to *trial*. If you are then so deeply insane that you are making no sense at all – you don't know what happened, and can't even instruct a lawyer to defend you – there will usually be a mere "trial of the facts". The purpose of this is to decide whether you really were the killer and, if so, whether you are still dangerous and should be sent to a secure mental hospital.

> NOTE. A trial of the facts that captured public attention not long ago was one that never happened. Accusations were made that Greville Janner (later Lord Janner of Broadstone) had sexually abused children. Past opportunities to prosecute him having been missed, prosecution was considered again in 2015, but by that time he had dementia and was unfit to plead. The Director of Prosecutions decided that there was no point in having a trial of the facts, because there was no chance of his offending in the future and he wouldn't be sent to a secure hospital anyway. Clamour arose and this decision was reversed, but he died before a trial of the facts could take place. As a result he was never proved to be guilty of anything.

Nor will you be convicted of murder if, at the time of the *killing*, you suffered from insanity within the *M'Naghten Rules*. This version of insanity is of psychosis which is less severe than would render you "unfit to plead", but which will still prevent a guilty verdict. The verdict in this case will be one of "not guilty by reason of insanity", and this time you really will be sent for an indefinite period to a secure mental hospital.

NOTE. The *M'Naghten Rules* take their name from Daniel M'Naghten who, in 1843, intending to shoot Sir Robert Peel, shot his secretary instead. Because he was clearly insane, he was acquitted of murder and sent to a mental hospital. Queen Victoria was unamused by this outcome, thinking it unduly lenient, and in the end the judges of the common law courts were asked to formulate a legal test of insanity. According to them an accused is legally insane if "labouring under such a defect of reason, from disease of the mind, as not to know the nature and quality of the act he was doing, or, if he did know it, that he did not know he was doing what was wrong." Believe it or not, this ungrammatical and unscientific test is still applied today. As time went on, clinicians found it increasingly nonsensical but, instead of replacing it, the authorities left it alone and came up with the defences of "partial insanity" described below.

Up to now we've considered three different mental states, but we're not done yet because there are still more that the court is supposed to be able to recognise and distinguish from those and from one another. The first two will get your murder charge reduced to manslaughter, and the severity of your sentence reduced along with it, if you can show that they affected you at the time of the *killing*.

One of these is "diminished responsibility". The present

definition of this was introduced by section 52 of the Coroners and Justice Act 2009 and I'm not setting it out in full here, but one of the things it says is this:

> If you were *caused* to do the killing by an "abnormality of mental functioning which … arose from a recognised medical condition" and fulfils certain criteria, then you will be acquitted of murder but convicted of manslaughter.

Think about this. It is the clearest statement of determinism. If the killing is caused – actually *caused* – by your abnormal mental functioning, then it is that abnormality and nothing else which makes it happen. That is what determines it. Forgive me for labouring this point: I do so because this is such a clear demonstration of the law's ability to snatch free will out of the jaws of determinism. The thinking behind this bit of law must be that your culpability is reduced by your faulty mental functioning, so you should be punished less severely – or, to put it another way, your free will (which, if it were complete, would lead to a murder conviction) is somehow incomplete, so your culpability is somehow also incomplete. But this is an impossible piece of sophistry and there's no logic to it. If the killing was actually caused by the abnormality, your culpability, if it existed at all, would be not reduced but obliterated, and you don't deserve to be *punished*. Nor is punishment going to deter you from further crime: what you need is psychiatric treatment, given in a secure hospital if need be. The same illogic did for poor Mr Meah in *Meah* v. *McCreamer*: his violent criminality was caused by his head injury, but he still spent a long time in gaol because of it.

The other mental state that reduces murder to manslaughter is one in which you "lose control". It originates in sections 54 and 55 of the 2009 Act and replaces the previous law about "provocation". It applies if the killing "resulted from … loss of self-control" which was "triggered" in one of several specified ways. Surely this raises all the same problems as "diminished responsibility": if the triggering event is such that you cannot control yourself, how are you culpable? But there's another interesting point here because this defence will succeed only if a normal person of your "sex and age" (wording that assumes, perhaps controversially, that the sexes differ from one another in their capacity for self-control) "might have reacted in the same or in a similar way". So if you did what any normal person might have done, you're still going to be punished for manslaughter. Why? Because you failed to exercise your free will in order to behave *better* than any normal person might have done. Make sense of this if you can.

NOTE. In these circumstances, you no more deserve to be punished than do any of the other people who might have done just as you did in the same situation. But deep in the human psyche lies the belief that if harm is done to someone, someone else must suffer for it. Normally the someone else is the person who did the harm – even though (as in this case) they cannot be considered culpable, even on the law's own terms, for doing it. So deep is this belief, however, that it sometimes leads to results that are absurd. In his book *The Stubborn System of Moral Responsibility* Bruce Waller re-tells the true story of the Russian village in which the blacksmith was found guilty of a brutal murder. Unfortunately the villagers had no other blacksmith and his services were indispensible, but they had an oversupply of tailors, who numbered seven in all, so they hanged one of them instead. And in my home county of Devon, a nineteenth century jury found a young man guilty of stealing hay, adding a note which said, "We don't think the prisoner done it, but there's been a lot of hay taken hereabouts by someone." Still more remarkable is the practice of inflicting savage punishment – hanging, burning at the stake, live burial, mutilation – on animals for behaving, to the detriment of humans, simply in accordance with their natures. According to a story in a July 2023 issue of *Private Eye*, this practice has not died out. In Aduel County, Sudan, a ram killed a woman by repeatedly headbutting her. Traditional leaders ruled that the ram be handed over to the victim's family as "blood compensation", but not before it had suffered three years' imprisonment at a military camp by way of punishment.

For our final illustration, let's return for a moment to the sentencing guidelines, where we can note that one of the mitigating factors is "the fact that the offender suffered from any mental disorder or mental disability which (although not [amounting to diminished responsibility]) lowered the offender's degree of culpability." There are of course other mental conditions in the guidelines which a court is thought capable of assessing, such as sadism, sexuality, racial or religious hostility, premeditation and so on.

So in the case of murder there are well over seven distinct mental states, each with its own definition and each to be found only by probing the often inaccessible mind of the killer. Lawyers have a maxim, "The devil himself knoweth not the mind of man", but obviously it doesn't apply here. And let's cut to the chase: what all this boils down to is the idea of moral responsibility grounded in the idea of free will. I don't believe in either of these things, but they do exist as concepts, and those who created the justice system must have believed in them – and believed, moreover, that they could exist as percentages of themselves, split into different bits of different sizes so as to "justify" different degrees of culpability and punishments of differing severity. Is this even theoretically possible? Even if free will existed, would it be meaningful to say that you possess only seventy per cent. of it and so are only seventy per cent culpable? Surely not. Free will, were it to exist, would not be a *thing*. You can have big and small helpings of a pudding, but not of free will.

By concentrating on defects in the law of murder, I don't want to give the impression that defects are not to be found in the rest of the criminal law, because of course they are. Take one random example. If Mr. McCreamer's bad driving had killed Mr Meah instead of injuring him, Mr. McCreamer might have found himself charged with causing death by dangerous driving. Now suppose that Mr. Meah was not a casual acquaintance, but a relative or a close friend of Mr. McCreamer. Should this make a difference to the sentence? Surely not, but it does. Are you guessing that it increases the sentence? If so, you're wrong: it reduces it. Does the Sentencing Council (whose guidance this is) think that drivers' culpability is reduced because they would suffer worse regret and, with it, greater *self*-punishment, for killing a brother or a best buddy than for killing a toddler in a push chair? Your guess may be better than mine.

Adrian Raine, born in the United Kingdom, was a Professor several times over in the University of Pennsylvania when he published his book *The Anatomy of Violence: The Biological Roots of Crime* in 2013. It caused quite a stir, attracting not only wide coverage and favourable reviews, but a laudatory leading article in *The Times*. He showed that violent crime results from detectable brain abnormalities.

Chemical imbalances play a part, and violence may result from faulty genetic endowment, particularly if combined with destructive upbringing. These findings advance our knowledge of how violent crime is determined, putting more emphasis on nature than on nurture. Did those responsible for the criminal justice system modify it in the light of these findings? Of course not, and they couldn't have done so even if they had wanted to. Over the years they have tried to take account of scientific developments while still preserving the public's belief in free will and culpability. This endeavour is already producing nonsensical results. To pursue it any further would strain creativity, and credulity, past breaking point.

I'd like to leave the last word to a lawyer, Sean Daly, writing in 2015 in the *Nevada Law Journal*:

> The theory of retribution rests on the public's erroneous conception of free will, and perpetuates moral confusion. Furthermore, by instituting retribution as a legitimate punishment, we waste our scientific and legal efforts on creating spurious distinctions in responsibility when we should be evaluating the efficacy of, and enhancing, our other theories of punishment. Thus, as Roscoe Pound wrote in 1922, "in order to deal with crime in an intelligent and practical manner we must give up on the retributive theory."

FOURTEEN

Crime – sense and consistency

I hope I've managed to show that the criminal justice system is in fact unjust and incoherent. Whether I have or not, you may be asking, perhaps with asperity, why I've paid so much attention to criminals and so little to their victims. Never mind whether criminals deserve to be punished, you may say, what's important is that their victims don't deserve to be victims; and how right you would be. But the only way to reduce the number of victims is to reduce the number of crimes, and in order to do that we need to replace the idea of free will with a real understanding of criminality, and to act on that understanding. And this, unfortunately, is another piece of reality that humankind finds it very hard to bear although, again, it probably wasn't one that T.S. Eliot had in mind.

What Bernard Shaw wrote in *Caesar and Cleopatra* could stand as an only slightly exaggerated description of the present system, dominated as it is by retributory punishment:

> And so, to the end of history, murder shall breed murder, always in the name of right and honour and peace, until the Gods are tired of blood and create a race that can understand.

Sadly, understanding is often devalued. Sir John Major's comment about crime, made in 1993, has reached the *Oxford Book of Quotations*:

Society needs to condemn a little more and understand a little less.

Many people probably agreed with this populist comment, but I can't find an excuse for it. Perhaps he thought that to understand a crime was to let the criminal get away with it: I don't know. But how can you deal effectively with anything without understanding it? Anyway, he seems to have had something of a Damascene conversion, because in May 2023, thirty years on and now a knight of the realm, he made a speech in which he condemned various aspects of the justice system. Among other things, he said (and I paraphrase):

Petty criminals shouldn't be in prison at all because there are better alternatives: community service, rehabilitation, care and medical treatment. These alternatives are more effective and more fair than short sentences, including those imposed on low-level drug dealers (likely to be of "limited intelligence as well as being addicts themselves"). Imprisoning people who are incapable of self-control is simply wrong because they require care and not incarceration. Mentally ill prisoners who are violent should be held securely, but "they too require care as well as custody". Responsibility for those who are not violent should pass to the Department of Health and Social Care because they need "the most effective and humane punishment".

That last point is particularly important because the majority of prisoners are in fact mentally ill in one way or another (and very many wouldn't be in prison if they weren't).

Rory Stewart, as prisons minister, described prisons as "grotesque, horrifying and shameful" and, for young men sharing cells with those who were older and often mentally disturbed, defecating in front of one another, as producing "a horrifying combination of loneliness and terror". The scandal of the IIP prisoners, already mentioned, still continues, inflicting a hopelessness that leads some of them to self-mutilate. In the general prison population, one prisoner self-harms every nine and a half minutes. Rehabilitation is relatively rare and reoffending is frequent. Often people who go to prison for the first time, and could be reformed, come out hardened and primed to embark on a lifetime of serious crime. As the one-time Home Secretary, Douglas Hurd, has put it:

Prisons are expensive places for making bad people worse.

No one who cares about the justice system has any doubt of its cruelty, destructiveness, wastefulness and abject failure. But few people do care, and most politicians are among those who don't. This is partly because it would cost a lot to change the system, but mainly because an undercurrent of free will belief runs beneath all our feelings about it. People are in prison, so it is said, because they could and should, and really might, have run their lives better than they did. It's their own fault. Most people care about them no more than Philip Marlowe cared about Madder. But what might we say if we understood that it isn't their own fault – that it's a fault in them, no doubt, but not a self-created fault? This is the question I want to consider in this chapter. Of course it's true that, even if the avowed purposes of the present system remained unchanged, they could still be implemented in a hugely better way, so as to produce hugely better results. This is what Sir John Major was saying in his speech. But suppose that the system itself could be changed: what then? If all I've been trying to say up to now were to be generally accepted – all right, this is just a hypothesis – how might the justice system be modified in the light of it?

Cast your mind back, if you will, to the five aims of sentencing prescribed in the Sentencing Act 2020 and set out in the previous chapter. There's nothing wrong in principle with the last four, but the first one – retributory punishment – has to go. There's everything wrong with that one because it depends on the idea of free will and that idea is moonshine. I realise of course that, as of now, this change would be bitterly opposed by the general public and, because of that fact (and whether or not they opposed it themselves), by the politicians who would have the power to make it. To most people, retribution and justice are synonymous: retribution is what justice *is*; take it away and there is no justice; and to dispense with retribution is to dispense with the whole idea of deservedness. To me, retributory justice is a contradiction in terms – what could be just or moral about inflicting pain on someone for doing what they're programmed to do? – but a huge recalibration of the moral compass would be required if that view were to be generally accepted.

And yet, and yet – there's always this strange paradox: that despite our belief in free will, we believe also in determinism. Determinism is always there, accepted implicitly, hiding in the plainest of plain sight, the elephant in the room that we know about but never see. Not long ago there was a series of television programmes called *Britain's Most Evil Killers*. Its description begins:

> True crime series that examines some of the most notorious murderers in the United Kingdom. Each episode focuses on an infamous case in Britain, and looks into *what exactly drove the killers to commit their crimes.*

The claim implicit in the italicised words (the italics are mine, of course) seems over-ambitious, to put it mildly: if it were possible to show "exactly" what drove someone to commit a crime, it would involve a full examination of their biological inheritance and their past life, and it couldn't be done in the course of a television programme. But the claim itself is a clear endorsement of determinism. It flatly contradicts any idea that criminals are not driven at all, but are simply indulging in an inexplicable expression of free will. Yet no one who has read this description of the programme will have found it odd or objectionable. Two recent book titles convey a similar message: *The Mind of a Murderer: What Makes a Killer* and *The Making of a Monster,* this second one about the police officer, David Carrick. Its blurb says, "How did a popular boy from Salisbury grow up to become one of the country's most prolific rapists?" No one will have objected that killers and monsters make themselves, or suggested that killers kill and rapists rape only because they have free will. And when Tony Blair promised to be "hard on crime and hard on the causes of crime", no one protested that a crime has no causes except a freely willed decision to commit it. In truth we know there's no free will, except when we don't want to know.

The way in which the present justice system misses the point is easily illustrated. In 2022, Jordan McSweeney sexually assaulted and murdered a woman on her way home after a night out. The prosecution said he acted with "savagery … almost impossible to believe". In mitigation, his counsel pointed out that he had had a troubled childhood: his mother was a drug addict, and his first memory of his father of was of him trying to drown her in the bath; he was expelled from school; and he became a drug dealer and then a bareknuckle fighter. The judge said that these experiences did not "begin to justify" what McSweeney had done. But to say that is to miss the point by some distance. Of course the experiences didn't *justify* what he had done. Nor did they require that he should receive some sort of *leniency* for what he had done. Their real relevance was that they – in conjunction, no doubt, with other factors – *caused* what he had done. But when it comes to sentencing, the law sets its face against causality.

McSweeny received a life sentence, required to serve a minimum term of 38 years before being considered for release. A leading article in *The Times* said that this term wasn't long enough: "[S]uch a heinous crime surely deserves the harshest punishment, a whole life order". In support of this view, the article said that he already had 28 convictions for 69 crimes (and actually he had already served nine prison sentences); but how is this support? Doesn't it rather suggest that the justice system had failed for years to get the measure of McSweeney – a mentally abnormal man if ever there was one, very likely one with an inborn brain abnormality of the kind identified in Adrian Raine's book mentioned in the previous chapter – and deal with him more effectively? The persistence of his criminality would certainly seem to mark it as a copybook example of determinism, but *The Times* didn't see it that way. To them it was all about his culpability – about the need for retribution – and its last words were, "He does not deserve to walk free". (On appeal, his minimum term was reduced from 38 years to 33.)

If we want to reduce crime, we can't do it merely by reforming the justice system. The main thrust would have to involve work in the community, and I say more about that later on. But a reformed justice system would nonetheless have an important part to play. I have some thoughts about this, but first there's a hurdle to be faced. Do we really *want* the justice system to be geared to the reduction of crime? The answer, you might think, is an unequivocal Yes. But do we want to do it even if we have to give up on free will and deservedness and retribution? Barbara Wootton was mentioned in my first chapter. Back in 1968 she took part in a television debate in the *Your Witness* series. The motion was:

The purpose of the criminal law is, and ought to be, the punishment of wickedness.

She opposed this motion, arguing that the real purpose should simply be the prevention of crime. But a majority of the "jury" voted against her and in favour of the motion. It's possible that a different jury would vote differently today, but I rather doubt it. What we have here is evidence that we prioritise the punishment of "wickedness" over the reduction of crime. Reducing crime is not our priority. I think it should be and, if rationality were to prevail, it would be. Perhaps most people really do disagree with me, and those people, if they started to read this book at all, will already have thrown it in the bin. But as for me and my house, we will, if not serve the Lord, then at least pursue what we see as good sense as best we can.

To reduce crime, of course we must oppose criminals. Have I disqualified myself from saying this? I've been hammering away at the idea of deservedness, seeking to show that criminals do not *deserve* to be punished. So what right do I think we have to punish them, or to treat them in any other way that they don't like, or to obstruct them at all? The answer is obvious: as I said earlier, the victims of crime don't deserve to be victims, so criminals must be taken in hand and dealt with somehow. Society must defend itself against the harm done by crime and, so far as I'm concerned, that's the end of the matter.

Some people have taken this question much more seriously, seeking moral justification, despite the truth of determinism, for what amounts to using criminals as a means to an end. In an earlier chapter I mentioned the work of the determinist philosopher Gregg Caruso and his book *Rejecting Retributivism*. In collaboration with another determinist philosopher, Derk Pereboom, he puts forward, and describes in the book, "The Public Health-Quarantine Model". This "draws on a comparison between treatment of dangerous criminals and treatment of carriers of dangerous diseases". Neither of these groups of people is morally responsible for their condition, but it is just as legitimate to confine violent criminals as it is to quarantine disease carriers. I have put this idea very simply: it is developed in detail and with great thoughtfulness, but it doesn't seem to me, as a non-philosopher, that any justification is really needed for tackling criminals beyond the purely pragmatic one: that if there is a conflict between them and the saving of society from pain and harm, they must be the losers.

But it still isn't their fault that they must lose, and the real question now is not whether they should be apprehended and brought to book – of course they should – but how they should be treated after that. At present the system is dominated by retributive punishment: by the idea free will and deservedness. If once we jettison this idea, we could recast the system in such a way as to reflect reality and, in doing so, to be an effective way of dealing with criminals and of reducing crime. Of the five statutory aims of sentencing mentioned in the last chapter, I've proposed that we discard the first one. I say no more about the last (making reparation), but it's obviously constructive, and creating dialogue between criminals and their victims is certainly important. That leaves us with deterrence; reform and rehabilitation; and protection of the public. In principle there's nothing wrong with these aims as aims: the trouble is that they aren't being achieved.

The first aim – deterrence – is troublesome. It covers both individual deterrence (deterring convicted offenders from committing future crimes), and general deterrence (deterring potential offenders from committing any crimes at all). Many offenders, if given a job, would probably never offend again, but to treat them simply by giving them a job would hardly conduce to general deterrence. It is nonetheless true that the best way to deter individual offenders from future offending is to reform and rehabilitate them. I'm not suggesting that this is always possible, but I am suggesting that, so far as convicted offenders are concerned, the idea that a taste of something nasty today will deter them from risking another dose of nastiness tomorrow, is proved false by the rather clear statisics. McSweeney had served nine prison sentences for 69 crimes before he committed his seventieth, and these numbers cover only the crimes of which he was convicted. In this respect and in others too, and *pace* Michael Howard, prison doesn't work.

Jason McSweeney's 28 convictions amounted by no means to a record, by the way. In July 2023, *The Times* reported that, because the prisons were so full

> [m]ore than half of "hyper-prolific" criminals' cases do not lead to prison sentences, despite offenders having already been convicted at least 45 times.

What a shocking thing. The sentences meted out to these offenders had already failed in their objective "at least 45 times", but never mind: sending them to prison just once more would surely have brought this dismal record of failure to an end, the long winter of our discontent suddenly made glorious summer. Isn't that right?

But what about general deterrence? It's probably true that

the threat of prison, or of some other unpleasant sanction, is needed now to prevent many people from committing crimes. But we don't seem to see this fact for what it is: a sign of our stark failure to be a rational and compassionate society – a sign that in our homes, our schools, our towns and cities, our groups and communities and institutions, on our streets and even in our police forces, there are nests of infection in which savagery is fostered, conscience is warped, and alienation and anti-social attitudes develop and fructify. In 2013 *The Times* carried an obituary of Professor Norman Kreitman. He was a psychiatrist and poet who became a philosopher and embraced determinism. One day Bishop Richard Holloway asked him how the lives of damaged young people in Glasgow could be changed. According to the obituary, Kreitman "responded briskly":

Change the determinants.

You don't need to be a determinist to know that he was right. You could even call this a staggering glimpse of the bleeding obvious. When Tony Blair promised to be tough on the causes of crime, he had at least diagnosed the problem even if he couldn't keep the promise. The causes remain as potent as ever. To tackle them properly would require a vast investment of time, money, energy, expertise and political will, and it isn't going to happen anytime soon. But that's what is needed. In the meantime we rely, without conspicuous success, on the idea of general deterrence.

Let's look at the third aim (protection of the public) before we concentrate on the second. It's obvious enough that dangerous offenders, almost by definition mentally abnormal whether or not they fall within some legal criterion, need to be confined while they remain dangerous, but confined in conditions that are not punitive and which, probably combined with psychiatric treatment, conduce to their becoming safe. Here I'm just endorsing what Sir John Major said in his speech; and, by the way, let us endorse *everything* in his speech: it's all good sense.

I think there's an analogy between meeting an escaped tiger that hasn't had a square meal for days and thinks that you would make a good one, and meeting a serial killer who hasn't done any killing for a while and thinks that killing you would satisfy his need. Either of these life forms might get shot if shooting them were the only way to protect you, and that can't be helped. But if the tiger survives, no one will blame it for behaving according to its natural propensities: it will probably be taken back to the zoo from which it escaped and confined there – but confined for public safety, not for punishment. And so it should be, surely, with the serial killer, behaving equally according to his natural propensities, needing to be confined but not deserving of punishment.

Some interesting things have been said about dangerous offenders. Adrian Raine has gone so far as to suggest that people with the brain defects that he identifies might be locked up, albeit in the most enjoyable conditions, in order to protect the public from the violent crimes they have not yet committed. (The philosopher Saul Smilansky has described the imposition of such conditions as "funishment", rather than punishment.) Raine records discussing this with Shami Chakrabarti, who disagreed, pointing out that if there would be "a huge cost to our way of life and to the kind of liberal democracy that I say we want to live in." I am instinctively on her side (and in any case I don't see how you would find the people with the abnormalities or make an uncontested diagnosis), but perhaps this is a question for future generations. So too is the question of whether *compulsory* neurointerventions – conditioning, brain surgery, drugs – should be permitted. In the film *A Clockwork Orange*, the main character is subjected to an extreme form of conditioning; in *One Flew Over the Cuckoo's Nest* a perfectly sane but rebellious patient is subjected to surgical lobotomy that destroys his rebelliousness; and Alan Turing accepted chemical castration, under threat of imprisonment for homosexual acts, and killed himself two years later. For myself, I hope that future generations will countenance these interventions, if at all, very rarely and under the strictest conditions.

So now: reform and rehabilitation. If we really do reject the idea of free will and deservedness, this has to be the aim that, like Ben Adhem's name, leads all the rest, replacing in that pole position the aim of retributive punishment. Rehabilitation is probably very difficult indeed in many cases and impossible in some. (I say "probably" because I suspect that we don't really know how difficult it is because we haven't tried hard enough to find out.) No two offenders are exactly the same and a range of resources would need to be in place in order to provide each one with a real prospect of reform and rehabilitation. Let me count the ways. Some need medical treatment, some psychiatry or psychotherapy. Some need education (many can't read), some the acquisition of skills through training. Some need to acquire a sense of self-worth perhaps by spending time in a therapeutic community (such as that at Grendon prison). Some need to be weaned off drugs. And whether these resources are provided for prisoners in prison, or for offenders in the community, they may need to be combined with help in the outside world. Some offenders need help with family problems, some with finding a job (and employers should be encouraged not to reject them: perhaps some kind of guarantee could be provided) or with finding somewhere to live. Some have problems within their communities and some may even need help to move elsewhere – or perhaps the communities themselves need intervention.

All this, you may say, is unrealistic: we don't provide this amount of help even for people who have (as yet) committed no crimes at all. And of course we don't, but of course we should: this is where the general deterrence of crime joins hands with the rehabilitation of criminals. All these resources and more should be available both to prevent crime and to reform criminals. But there's little chance of our deciding to reduce crime in these ways. We much prefer to see existing criminals as culpable and try to punish the culpability out of them, and to deter potential criminals by the threat of punishment to come. Never mind that these stratagems don't work: at least they give us emotional satisfaction.

I don't want to suggest that the present regime is wholly devoid of constructive and reformative measures because that wouldn't be true. Inadequate, ill-funded and isolated, they struggle to exist and to survive. A newspaper article in 2015 illustrates both their existence and the public opinion with which they often have to contend. It was about Whatton, a Nottinghamshire prison for sex offenders. According to the article, the prison governor "doesn't believe in evil" and directs all her efforts to the prevention of re-offending. This involves a sustained attempt to make paedophiles "feel better about themselves – because it works":

> [I]f you hate sex offenders, you only make them more dangerous. But if you can find it in your heart to think of them and help them to think of themselves as human beings worthy of a future, then you protect a child.

But the writer of the article goes on to describe this as "a horrible paradox", rather than a sensible and constructive approach, and expresses her own views in this way:

> I don't like "kindness" in connection with treatment of child molesters. Like anyone, I have no truck with "soft" options. I want to send them to hell, not group therapy in Nottinghamshire.

This mention of softness illustrates an important point. Popular belief has it that there are only two approaches to crime: being soft on it (which doesn't work) and being hard on it (which does). There is certainly a sense in which extreme hardness would do the job. If all sentences were whole life sentences, crime would certainly fall. So it would, and with less expense, if all criminals were executed on conviction: this is the point made, in relation to murderers, by the former Deputy Chairman of the Conservative Party. But neither of these options exists in a civilised country. (It was only in the mid-twentieth century that the Lord Chief Justice, Lord Goddard, told the Royal Commission on Capital Punishment that a murderer whom he considered to be quite clearly insane should nonetheless be hanged because his insanity was "one of the reasons why he should be out of the way". No one, I think, would take that view now, and few took it even then.) And the contrast between hardness and softness would be false even if it were meaningful. Measures perceived as soft are often not soft at all: group therapy, for instance, involves hard and disturbing work if it is to succeed. In his book, *Turning Over the Pebbles: a Life in Cricket and in the Mind*, the cricketer and psychoanalyst Mike Brearley writes of his time on the staff of a clinic devoted to in-patient group therapy for adolescents. One patient could not bear the tension and left; some months later he wrote from a juvenile prison saying how much he valued the work at [the clinic], but it had been harder to face his feelings there than to act them out outside and be punished in prison. He wanted to encourage people to stick it out at [the clinic].

In any case, the choice between hardness and softness is wholly false. Hardness of itself is not a good way to reduce crime: we've been over that ground already. The true contrast must be between what works and what doesn't.

Nor should it be assumed that the prison population should remain anything like as great as it is now. I mentioned earlier that the United Kingdom has the highest imprisonment rate in Western Europe. We've already agreed – at least I have – with Sir John Major that petty offenders shouldn't be in prison at all. Such reformative measures as may exist in gaol are not applied to them because their sentences are too short, and 63 per cent of them commit another offence within a year of release. In a very interesting and enlightened book called *Justice on Trial: Radical Solutions for a System at Breaking Point*, Chris Daw QC has suggested that no non-violent criminals should need to be in prison at all, because modern surveillance methods would allow them to be monitored in their own homes.

Let's just notice a few of what are, at the time of writing, the prison statistics for the most recent year: 11,224 cases of self-harm; 313 deaths (88 self-inflicted); 22,319 assaults; and 2,564 serious assaults (most by prisoners on one another, some by prisoners on staff). All these figures are higher than those for the previous year. The prison population stands at 88,000, and although many – but by no means all – of these prisoners *need* to be in gaol, none *deserves* to be. A former prison officer, Alex South, who has written a book,

Behind These Doors, refers in an interview to overcrowding and says:

> We are doing little more than warehousing people. The result is that we're delivering really poor regimes in many of our prisons, with prisoners locked up for 22 hours a day. In a nutshell, it's dangerous.

And surely to goodness, and as she would probably agree, it's also inhumane.

I've referred before to Professor Bruce Waller's book, *The Stubborn System of Moral Responsibility.* When it comes to sentencing, he contrasted the systems which exist in the United States and the United Kingdom, based as they are upon the idea of individual moral responsibility and the deservedness of punishment, with those in Scandinavian countries. Gregg Caruso has done the same. These go a long way towards being the kind of systems that I've tried to describe. Without ignoring the need to confine dangerous offenders, they imprison fewer people that we do and, by turning prisons into places of reconstruction, they reduce reoffending to a far greater degree. In an article in *The Atlantic,* Professor Doran Larson explains:

> This is all possible because, throughout Scandinavia, criminal justice policy rarely enters political debate. Decisions about best practices are left to professionals in the field who are often published criminologists and consult closely with academics. Sustaining the barrier between populist politics and results-based prison policy are media that don't sensationalize crime – if they report it at all.

Accuracy requires me to record, sadly, some darkening of this bright picture. At the time of writing, a right-leaning government in Sweden is planning to reverse the existing penal policy by trebling the number of prison places.

For us to introduce real and effective means of crime reduction without making any changes in the criminal law itself, or in trial procedure, would be a possibility, and it would certainly do a lot of good. But if we really were in search of a rational and constructive system we should have to go further. In the quote which ended the previous chapter, Sean Daly criticised the "spurious distinctions in responsibility" which characterise the legal approach to crime. The responsibility he's talking about is moral responsibility (or culpability or deservedness), and the distinctions he's talking about are those exemplified in that chapter. The present system is geared, as the old television programme acknowledged, to the punishment of wickedness. In assessing this wickedness, the law makes some concessions to the mental state of the offender, but these concessions are hopelessly inept. As Daly suggests, they are full of artificial distinctions, framed in black and white language that no mental health professional would recognise. They also set the bar too high, so that pure punishment is inflicted on thousands of prisoners who are mentally ill and would not otherwise be liable to prison at all. They are often grudging to the point of absurdity: we've already noticed, for example, that you will be sentenced for manslaughter even if your killing was "caused" by mental illness; and that the same will happen to you if you lost control in circumstances in which anyone like you might equally have lost it. And they fail to take proper account of abnormalities of the physical brain. There can be no solution to these problems within the present system. All criminals, whether or not they suffer from mental illness, suffer from past circumstance.

Barbara Wootton, in her book, *Crime and The Criminal*

Law, proposed a solution which was shot down by criminal lawyers too hidebound to consider it objectively, but which has a great deal to commend it. She suggested that the mental element in crime had "got into the wrong place". In her view the purpose of a criminal trial should be simply to establish whether or not the accused did the act in question, and that the assessment of their mental state should be left until after the verdict when it could be made comprehensively, with expert inter-disciplinary input and without regard to the artificiality of statutory distinctions. It would then be of crucial importance in deciding on the sentence to be imposed on the individual offender – as constructive a one as was consistent with public safety – and the conditions that should accompany it. The sentence would be based on a psychological, neurological and biological understanding of crime. The difference between "sane" and "mentally abnormal" criminals doesn't depend on one lot having free will and the other not, because neither has it. Nor does it depend on one lot deserving punishment and the other not, because neither does. It depends only on the differing ways in which they need to be treated. In Barbara Wootton's scheme, the trial itself would resemble the "trial of the facts", described in the previous chapter, which can take place when the accused is grossly insane, but without the drawbacks inherent in such trials, because in this case the accused would be able to mount a proper defence – instructing a lawyer, raising an alibi, giving explanations, and so on.

What's wrong with this idea? Lawyers looked down from a great height and condemned it without reserve. To them, the mental element could not possibly be ignored in a trial. If that happened, there would be no distinction between a robber who stabs you in order to relieve you of your wallet and a surgeon who cuts you open to relieve you of your malignant tumour. Believe it or not, this sort of objection is still made today. Not long ago I read a very good book by a retired judge of the Old Bailey: it's the one mentioned in Chapter 9. I was so taken with it, and with the understanding it showed of the factors that go to produce crime, that I wrote to the author and mentioned Barbara Wootton's ideas. This was a foolish thing to do because there was no chance that they would commend themselves to an Old Bailey judge, and of course they didn't. In the course of a very kindly reply the author said that

> without moral responsibility [being taken into account], the act may not be a crime – killing someone is no crime if it was a accident.

But there are obvious answers to objections like this. To begin with, no one even today is prosecuted unless it is in the public interest, and in the real world no one would prosecute the surgeon or the person involved in the accidental death. This is all the more obvious because, if they were to be prosecuted and convicted, the court would immediately release them – no sentence would be justified – so they wouldn't be prosecuted in the first place. If the law were ever changed so as to encompass Barbara Wootton's ideas, the changes would happen only in the context of a general understanding of their purpose.

As we come to the end of this chapter, let me quote some of what Winston Churchill said as Home Secretary in the House of Commons in 1910 – not because it isn't already well-known, nor because it isn't rather hackneyed, but just because it's Churchill and it may therefore be a little bit impervious to atavistic attack:

The mood and temper of the public in regard to the treatment of crime and criminals is one of the most unfailing tests of the civilisation of any country.... [T]ireless efforts towards the discovery of curative and regenerating processes and an unfaltering faith that there is a treasure, if only you can find it, in the heart of every person – these are the symbols which in the treatment of crime and criminals mark and measure the stored up strength of a nation, and are the sign and proof of the living virtue in it.

If this test of our civilisation is indeed valid, and it seems a pretty good one to me, then we are very much less civilised than we like to think.

FIFTEEN

Ending

I've tried to identify some aspects of reality that most of humankind, at this stage of our evolution, cannot bear. Of course there are others. Does it matter that they go unrecognised? Are they perhaps bound to go unrecognised? Just as we have built our physical environment in such a way as to accommodate our physical capacities – light switches within reach, cars needing no more than four limbs to drive them, chairs of the right size to fit the human bottom – so we have constructed our mental and moral landscape in such a way as to accommodate the mentality and the emotions with which we find ourselves (I was going to say lumbered) endowed. Any change in the current dispensation is bound to be gradual.

It is implicit in what I've written that I myself want it to change – want it so much that I've spent all this time slogging away at the book in the faint hope that it might just do something to encourage change. But I can't produce any rational argument for change. What does it matter if our species lives on in a delusional state? Certainly there is no objective sense in which it matters: if it matters at all, it can matter only to us, and if it doesn't matter to us, then it doesn't matter. In the general scheme of things, the fact that it matters to me is of no interest at all. But it does matter to me, and this is my book, so I can at least express some feelings about it. They come in two parts. There is, first, a fact that I find painful and shocking, something that came as a surprise to me when I started to grow up and to which I never really became reconciled: the fact that the present moral dispensation causes a great deal of unnecessary and unjustifiable suffering. If morality means anything at all, then our present moral stances are grossly immoral. You may dispute this as a fact, or you may accept it but not care about it: I've tried to demonstrate it earlier, and I'm not trying to prove anything here. The second set of feelings that move me personally has to do with human dignity and, for want of a better word, authenticity. I just don't like the idea that the human race cannot, and never will, face up to the realities of its existence.

Authenticity? Perhaps I am stepping outside my main theme in expressing a wish for this. I think – no, I feel – that it must somehow be a bad thing if, for example, we lived our lives unknowingly in a world generated as a computer simulation; or if, like the bulk of the population in Aldous Huxley's *Brave New World*, we were born in hatching trays and lived in a scientifically engineered world kept happy and contented by doses of the drug Soma, with the Savage almost the only person still living outside this artificial construction. All such situations represent an inauthenticity, a retreat from reality, but I can't prove that this would be a bad thing: those whom such unrealities had engulfed would know no other reality and would probably be no less "happy".

I read somewhere about a survey carried out in America. Members of the public were asked how much effort they thought it was worth expending in order to preserve a species called *homo sapiens*. Most people thought it wasn't worth expending much at all. They didn't realise that they themselves were members of this species, and who can blame them? If you don't happen to know that the human race is called *homo sapiens*, you probably wouldn't guess. Even if you knew that *sapiens* is the Latin for sapience or wisdom, you still might not guess because this is a self-interested accolade awarded to the species by its own members, and it's hardly an accurate description.

Might it be more accurate to call it a lousy species? When, in a despairing moment, I first wondered whether we might be better described in that way, I dismissed the idea – not because the description seemed too harsh, but because it seemed meaningless. There is no comparator, no other human species compared with which we could be called lousy. We are the only one there is, I said to myself, so get used to it. But then it struck me that actually there is a comparator: not a real one, but one that lives in the imaginations of some of us. It's the species that isn't irrational, ignorant, credulous, uncomprehending, self-defeating, ill at ease with its sexuality, mired in its contradictory beliefs, impelled by a savagery let loose by misperception and misunderstanding. Could this imaginary species ever become a real one? Could our species ever become that species?

Bertrand Russell didn't mince words when he described *homo sapiens*:

> I hate the world and almost all the people in it ... even the pacifists who keep saying human nature is essentially good, in spite of daily proofs to the contrary. I hate the human race – I am ashamed to belong to such a species.

Even if we wanted to transform ourselves, we couldn't do it. We can't shrug off what circumstance has made us, as a snake sheds its skin. If you believe in free will, you should be contradicting me here. You should be saying, with Barack

Obama, "Yes we can". But you know we can't, and most of us don't want to. If change in the current dispensation is to come about at all, it will indeed happen gradually, over any generations there may be still to come. But my point of view is not unique to me. There are many other people saying some of the same things. They will keep at it and probably others will join them. The American president, Calvin Coolidge, was by all accounts a taciturn and undemonstrative man – so much so that when Dorothy Parker, the great American writer and humourist, was told that he had died, she said, "How can they tell?" But he stirred himself to say something about persistence:

> Nothing in this world can take the place of persistence. Talent will not; nothing is more common than unsuccessful people with talent. Genius will not; unrewarded genius is a proverb. Education will not; the world is full of educated failures. Persistence and determination alone are omnipotent.

The persistence required to bring about a general disbelief in free will and moral responsibility would be huge, and all the more so because I think there is, even in us disbelievers, a small residual urge to believe. Being in a small way a human being myself, I can't claim to *like* the fact that the cruellest people among us do not deserve punishment. A bit of me revolts at the idea. But (as my father would have said, as he said about so many things, though he probably wouldn't have said it about this one) – there it is. And if I waver, I am strengthened by something else that Bertrand Russell said, this time in an interview:

> When you are studying any matter, or considering any philosophy, ask yourself only: "What are the facts and what

is the truth that the facts bear out?" Never let yourself be diverted, either by what you would wish to believe, or by what you think would have been the efficient social effects if it were believed, but look only and surely at: "What are the facts?".

Rather deliberately, I've been describing human beings as a species. We are indeed just one among the very many species on the planet, like all of them an accidental product of evolution, and sharing nearly 99 per cent. of our DNA with chimpanzees. Unlike bears and chimpanzees, we no longer shit in the woods (although I was impelled to do so once, in circumstances not worth recalling) but we do still shit as every other animal does. Bears and chimpanzees also die in the woods, and we seldom do that, but we all die somewhere and that's the end of us, as death is the end of the other animals. Too often we see ourselves as Something Completely Different. Of course we are unique in having established what we call a civilisation, and a complex and sophisticated one at that, and in gaining dominance over all the other animals, but we are still ourselves an animal species. In our drive towards some sort of effulgence, we have done great harm to other species, and even to many members of our own, and we have shied away from many of the realities of our existence, creating illusions not shared or needed by any of our fellow creatures. I keep thinking of words "only man is vile" in the hymn written by Bishop Reginald Heber (1783-1836):

What tho' the spicy breezes
Blow soft o'er Ceylon's isle;
Though every prospect pleases,
And only man is vile?

But I think he wasn't attributing vileness to humankind in general, as he might have been, but only to the non-Christian inhabitants of Ceylon (who typify "[T]he heathen in his blindness [who] bows down to wood and stone") because he goes on, in what might today be thought a remarkable piece of arrogance:

> Shall we, whose souls are lighted
> With wisdom from on high,
> Shall we to men benighted
> The lamp of life deny?
> Salvation! O Salvation!
> The joyful sound proclaim,
> Till earth's remotest nation
> Has learned Messiah's name.

And so absorbed another piece of exceptionalism, another bit of unreality.

It begins to look to me as if what I'm hankering for is something called truth. Do you gain access to truth by accepting reality? Surely you do. It would be hard to find two more disparate artistic creations than *Four Quartets* and the film *A Few Good Men*, but when T.S. Eliot's bird said that humankind cannot bear very much reality, it must have been saying rather the same thing as the Jack Nicolson character said to the Tom Cruise character at the climax of the film: "You can't handle the truth". This idea that the truth can't be handled is surely what underlies the modern tendency to censor writings that are seen – at least by those who do the censoring – as upsetting. For example, in August 2022 *The Times* reported that

> Universities have started removing books from reading lists to protect students from "challenging" content and have applied trigger warnings to more than 1,000 texts.

Many other recent initiatives of this kind have been taken with the same end in view: that of ensuring that painful feelings lie dormant, a happier world of make-believe is preserved, the truth is hidden, and change is discouraged – all of this, surely, with just the same purpose as the administration of Soma in Huxley's *Brave New World*.

When, towards the end of his life, Freud completed his book *Moses and Monotheism*, he made a comment that merged his thoughts about religious truth with those about truth in general:

> The religious argument is based on an optimistic and idealistic premise. The human intellect has not shown itself elsewhere to be endowed with a very good scent for truth, nor has the human mind any special readiness to accept truth.

Francis Bacon's Essay on Truth, published in 1597, starts by recalling the biblical story of Jesus brought for trial before Pontius Pilate:

> "What is truth?", said jesting Pilate, and would not stay for an answer.

And perhaps he was wise not to stay, because there seems to be no general agreement among philosophers about what "truth" really is. But we do know what it is, don't we – know well enough to serve our everyday purposes? *The Washington Post* knows enough about truth to record that during his presidency Donald Trump uttered 30,573 lies and misleading statements. (This is not counting the ones uttered before his presidency and those still being uttered now.)

When I was a young child, my father told me with great seriousness that I must always tell the truth and that no harm would come to me if I did so. He can hardly have meant this as advice to which I should adhere throughout my life – that would have verged on insanity – but even as a piece of advice to a child it had its shortcomings. I didn't turn out to be the son he wanted, and in an attempt to conceal this from him I sometimes felt the need to tell him lies. Conventional wisdom would have it that he was at fault, because he should have valued me for the different person I was and for the different ideas I harboured. But that would have been a hard thing to do: it is difficult to value views opposed to your own.

In a famous biblical quotation (John, 8:32) Jesus said:

Ye shall know the truth, and the truth shall make you free.

This quote has gone round the world, adorning various seats of learning, as though it were a general injunction to seek the truth wherever it may be found, but Jesus didn't mean it that way. The only truth he thought likely to produce freedom was the truth of his own teachings, and he made this statement to "those Jews who believed in him".

My stream of consciousness bears me next to Sir John Betjeman's poem *Christmas*, of which one verse goes:

And is it true? And is it true,
This most tremendous tale of all,
Seen in a stained-glass window's hue,
A Baby in an ox's stall?
The Maker of the stars and sea
Become a Child on earth for me?

Not from where I'm standing it isn't, but this at least is a *questioning* of the truth – a seeking of the truth despite what must surely be an urge to find it where you want it to be. Although he had no time for religion, Bertrand Russell might have been mildly approving, because of course very few people (and very few philosophers, as I've already suggested) are really open-minded when they come to consider the truth. They don't really look for it: they just flourish their own versions of it.

As I come towards the end of this book (and indeed towards the end of my own existence, because surely there can't be much more of that either) what I think I want to say more than anything else is this. All the people in the world are members of a single species, all of us are creatures of circumstance, and we differ from one another, in mind and body, only because our circumstances have differed. If this rather obvious fact were to be generally absorbed, some sort of transformation might surely begin to take place. Some people are, by any standard, disgusting, and you certainly don't have to like them or to put up with them, but you might still be able to see that it isn't their fault. When the German intellectual Hans Magnus Enzenberger died in November 2022, an obituary quoted him as saying, about the crimes of the Third Reich:

We know we are to blame, and that it is not our fault that we are to blame.

Those more knowledgeable than me may know exactly what he meant by this, but if he meant what I think he meant then his statement chimes perfectly with what I'm trying to say. If we behave badly, it is true that we are to blame for doing what we do, but only in the sense that we are instrumental in the doing of it (as we might say that the weather is to blame for the failure of the crops). And it is also true that this reveals a fault in us, but only in the sense that nature and nurture have not combined to make us better people. This fault is in us, but it is not our fault that we have it.

Before, as his doctor said of the life of King George V just before it ended (or the doctor himself ended it), I draw peacefully to a close, let me attempt a quick summary of my earlier chapters. Our rationality is certainly limited and often bogus. Our consciences are not infallible pointers to goodness. Our savagery towards "the others" is never assuaged. Our religious belief is just a piece of human exceptionalism. We are still not reconciled to the realities of death. Our perceptions of other people (and indeed of ourselves) are nearly always faulty in one way of another. Our attitude towards sexuality is a strange mixture of titillation and condemnation. Our belief in free will is as nonsensical as it is harmful as it is prevalent. Much the same must be said of our belief in moral responsibility. And our attitude to crime and criminals is the sad, bad and unconstructive result of nearly all these other faults and inadequacies.

I'd love to see them all disappear, but of course that won't happen for many years to come, if it ever does. My father fought in the First World War, so let me attempt a little retrospective reconciliation by quoting from one of its songs, which perhaps he sang and which seems apposite here: "There's a long, long trail a-winding into the land of my dreams." I'm sure he had his dreams, even if they were not what my dreams are. I sometimes wonder what he was dreaming as he lay dying for month after month in his bed at the top of the house. I think he saw no need for the world to change its ways, whereas I myself identify more closely with the experience of the three wise men in T.S. Eliot's poem *Journey of the Magi,* when they came back from their travelling to Bethlehem ("A cold coming we had if it, just the worst time of the year for a journey, and such a long journey"), having made their offerings to the Christ child:

We returned to our places, these Kingdoms
But no longer at ease here, in the old dispensation,
With an alien people clutching their gods.
I should be glad of another death.

PRAISE FOR 'THE NONSENSE OF FREE WILL'

Endorsements

"There are philosophical, scientific, scholarly, novel, determined, American, pompous, dotty and other books on free will and determinism. There are also a few books that are lucid and informal introductions for ordinary readers and let you know that your free will does not exist. Richard Oerton's may be the best of these." – *Ted Honderich, Grote Professor Emeritus of the Philosophy of Mind and Logic, University College London*

"This book is superbly written and a delight to read. Starting as a clearly reasoned treatment of determinism, it merges seamlessly into a critique of English criminal law and penal policy, and ends with a plea for society to abandon what the author sees as its irrational belief in free will." – *Joshua Rozenberg, Q.C., legal commentator, formerly legal editor of The Daily Telegraph*

"This fascinating book explains and discusses one of the most difficult questions underlying criminal liability – are we right to work on the basis that all sane people can exercise 'free will'? Richard Oerton explores the free will v. determinism debate with remarkable and rare clarity. This is not a book only for academics: it is of vital interest to all who want to think about the way society is organised." – *Dr. Stephen Cretney, D.C.L., F.B.A., Q.C., LL.D., Emeritus Fellow of All Souls College, Oxford*

Reviews

"This is a terrific book ... so clear and readable that it would be appropriate for general readers, introductory philosophy courses, and undergraduate courses in criminal justice and the humanities." – *Richard Double, Emeritus Professor of Philosophy, University of Pennsylvania*

"What I loved about your book [is that you] have an unsurpassed grasp of the deep issues in free will and reach the most reasonable conclusions, without becoming sidetracked by the philosophical jargon that impedes professional philosophers." – *Professor Double, in a personal communication*

"What Richard Dawkins did for atheism, Richard Oerton has here done for determinism: he has taken those doubts about the existence of free will – all those unspoken blasphemous thoughts so many of us secretly harbour – and distilled them into an intelligent, accessible and highly engaging polemic. I would urge anyone with any doubts about free will to read this book; to read one's own inchoate ideas expressed in such a clear and concise manner is simply exhilarating. After many years of contemplation, The Nonsense of Free Will has provided the encouragement I needed to finally accept determinism and its implications, and I suspect that there will be many others for whom this book will have had a similar effect." – *Benjamin Langlois*

"Oerton has written a terrific book, a must read for anyone interested in the free will debate and why it matters. He reaches all the right conclusions, for the right reasons, stated most felicitously ... a delightful read – unassuming, straightforward, informed and funny" – *Tom Clark, Director of the Center for Naturalism, U.S.A.*

"I have read a fair amount about this subject. Much of it has been excellent. But nothing I ever read got to the core of things the way Oerton does. No-one ever made their case with such a combination of simplicity and surgical precision. Free will is a vast issue. Vast and slippery and mysterious. To tackle it is no small undertaking. Oerton, however, makes it seem easy. He demystifies free will. " – *Stephen Campana*

"Every summer I try to introduce undergraduates who are thinking about choosing the criminology, sentencing and penal system course to some 'holiday' reading that will get them thinking ... Had I read this book in time, it would definitely have been on the list. It will be there next year. This is a thoughtful and thought-provoking book." – *Professor Loraine Gelsthorpe, Cambridge University*

Other reviews on Amazon

"A very clear and fair account of the problems associated with the concept of free will. Whatever your views are before reading you will be much better informed after finishing this book"

"... a brilliant achievement and a triumphant piece of scholarly writing"

"I ... was truly taken aback by the clarity and simplicity with which Oerton approaches this cloudy subject ... a fantastic writer and a straight communicator"

" ... most people will gain a tremendous amount of insight from reading this book"

"If you are looking for an easy to read yet powerful explanation of the determinism v. free will contest then I strongly recommend this book"

"… presents clear, precise arguments that are well structured and persuasive … should leave you wondering why you believed in free will in the first place and with a whole new perspective on life" "I absolutely loved [this] book"

"An easy to read and understand, fun and well written argument for the nonsense of free will"

" … a fantastic addition to the growing literature about how we interpret a world without free will … Since it is free of excessive philosophy jargon the text is very accessible for those new to the topic and still rich and rewarding for those more familiar. A 'must read' …"

"Highly recommended" "Wonderfully written and – to my mind – totally persuasive"

"Nice perspective from someone familiar with the legal system … honest, refreshingly human, and full of good sense."

"This is one of the best, balanced and fair books which show 'free will' for what it really is, a nonsense idea. Nonsense, in that it can't even be mapped on to reality"

"Brilliantly explained"

"Thought the book was nonsense!"

PRAISE FOR 'THE CRUELTY OF FREE WILL'

Endorsements

"Oerton has done it again: a delightful, wise and compassionate diagnosis of the free will error, and why correcting it matters so much." – *Tom Clark, Director of the Center for Naturalism, U.S.A.*

"The Cruelty of Free Will contains an unpretentious and heartfelt denial of the sort of free will that supports retribution, whether championed by compatibilists, libertarians or illusionists. Oerton's denial of free will places itself squarely in the determinist, materialist and atheist traditions. His denunciation of moral responsibility is so straightforward yet profound that even those who are most strongly committed to this idea may feel impelled to rethink their attachment. Highly recommended for anyone who has ever been tempted to assign 'just deserts' – that is, for everyone." – *Richard Double, Emeritus Professor of Philosophy, University of Pennsylvania*

"On a large subject about which there is common belief, good sense is rare. So is amiable lucidity. And humanity. This book has them." – *Ted Honderich, Grote Professor Emeritus of the Philosophy of Mind and Logic, University College London*

"Moral responsibility and just deserts promote human dignity, protection of the innocent, equal opportunity, and respect for individual rights: or so both philosophers and "the folk" generally believe. That deep conviction makes it essential to preserve belief in moral responsibility at all costs. Richard Oerton demolishes that belief with wit, insight, and clarity, and this demolition work clears the ground for building a more humane and decent and scientifically sound system." – *Bruce Waller, Professor of Philosophy, Youngstown State University*

Reviews

"The Cruelty of Free Will is Richard Oerton's follow-up to The Nonsense of Free Will. The discussion of free will is often convoluted and frequently full of hostility. It does not need to be and Oerton does a great job of explaining the problems with free will as it is generally accepted in the West. ... [F]ree will says in response to any given situation ... that we are completely free to make any choice. Yet in every aspect of our daily lives we rely on determinism to get us through ... If we ... [thought] that any given action another person took was not determined by their make-up and their history then we would be in a completely random and chaotic world. Any field that looks for reasons behind a person's actions relies on determinism, not free will, being the driving force. Free will is what stands behind many of society's cruellest and least compassionate norms and laws. If that poor person had chosen better they would not be poor, so they are to blame ... Criminals should be punished because they freely chose their path ... This isn't to say criminals should not be held accountable, they should. But retribution rather than rehabilitation is preferred because people believe the criminal chose freely to follow the path they took ... I want to include this extended quote from [a summary written by Oerton]:

> "We cling to the idea of free will because we're still a savage species. You won't have liked some of my earlier assertions and you certainly won't like this one – but surely it's true.

Evolution has not (yet) produced in us a species dedicated to the general welfare of its own members or with any strong inhibitions against killing, harming or exploiting them. (If you doubt this, pick up a newspaper.) We are still a savage species, and free will belief lets some of it out of the cage in which, most of the time, civilisation confines it."

– *Earl Messer on Amazon.com, NetGalley, Goodreads and LIbraryThing*

Other reviews on Amazon and Goodreads

"[A] part of the growing data that indicates the popular notion of 'free will' is a myth indeed. A … truth that Americans especially will find hard to swallow."

"He makes lots of good points about free will being nonsense and cruel by its very being. I agree. It's a total set up."

"The author is both clear and concise, a rarity in those who write about philosophical conceptions."